SPIRITUAL DISCIPLINES SERIES

SPIRITUAL STORYTELLING

Discovering and Sharing Your Spiritual Autobiography

A SMALL GROUP DISCUSSION GUIDE

RICHARD PEACE

with
JENNIFER HOWE PEACE

NAVPRESS
BRINGING TRUTH TO LIFE
NavPress Publishing Group
P.O. Box 35001, Colorado Springs, Colorado 80935

Pilgrimage Publishing, Hamilton, Massachusetts

ISBN 08910-98984

Cover illustration: Wood River Gallery

Printed in the United States of America

1 2 3 4 5 6 7 8 9 10 / 99 98 97 96

Contents

Acknowledgments

I first learned about the power of sharing our stories while an undergraduate at Yale. During my final year I became a member of what was called a Senior Society. Senior Societies were the descendants of the old Yale Debating Societies. They consisted of small groups of men (Yale was not yet co-ed) who met together on a regular basis. The activities of each group were kept private, but in our group (as in others, I suspect) one of the things we did was to tell our stories to one another. This was a powerful experience for me. It was a time of self-discovery. It was a time in which I began to discover the humanity of others outside my own circle. Up to that point my friends had been drawn mainly from Yale Christian Fellowship (an InterVarsity chapter). But now I was the only "religious" person in the group. (I later learned that this was one reason why I was selected for membership in this Senior Society—to represent a religious viewpoint.)

I came to appreciate in wholly new ways these other men who were so different from me. It was a warm appreciation, not one of judgment. Up to that time I had a fairly strong "us/them" mentality: "us" being the good-guy Christians; "them" being the worldly others. I learned how diverse our stories were. I learned how everyone struggled and everyone cared. Yes, I was the "Christian" in the group, but I was certainly not the only one with a sense of God or a desire to be good and to do right. I also learned about the power of telling our stories to one another: how this bound us together in our diversity. It was very difficult to dislike or disdain people whose stories I knew.

Many years later, when I designed a course at Gordon-Conwell Theological Seminary called "The Pursuit of Wholeness," I revived this idea of sharing life stories. I asked the students to organize themselves into small groups of five or six. After some preliminary sharing and group-building, each student was given one small group session in which to share his or her spiritual autobiography. At the conclusion of each presentation, the group responded to the story. This small group exercise immediately proved to be deeply meaningful. Consistently over the years, the evaluations rated this experience near the top of what students most appreciated about the course.

It is this experience that forms the background of *Spiritual Storytelling*. This book is the product of the fifteen years I have taught "The Pursuit of Wholeness." I am indebted to the feedback I have received from my students. In this book I have amplified the whole experience. The course handout which describes how to write a spiritual autobiography has become the long middle section of this book. I believe that I have provided far more detailed instructions than I gave to my students.

Likewise, I have added the Bible studies on Abraham. The story of his pilgrimage contains many elements of a spiritual autobiography. He had his good times when he proved himself to be a faithful and reliable friend of God. But he also had his bad times (which are more frequent) when he proved himself to be weak, fearful, inadequate, obstinate, sinful, and mean. In other words, he is no plastic saint whose perfection is forever beyond us. On the contrary, he struggles just as we all do. He also encounters God. Right from the beginning he knows that he is called by God to a special task. His story is marked by the presence of God, despite his many inadequacies. So too our stories. We are not called to the awesome task of founding a nation that will become the people of God. But we are called to other tasks, all part of the Kingdom building that God is doing. Our stories, like Abraham's story, bears the imprint of God. It is my hope that the studies in the life of Abraham will help you to prepare a more perceptive rendering of your own story. I used a number of traditional resources in preparing the Bible studies, including Bible dictionaries, an atlas, and several studies about Abraham. The most helpful resources were four commentaries:

- *Genesis* (the *Interpretation* series) by Walter Brueggemann. Atlanta: John Knox Press, 1982.
- *Genesis 1–15* and *Genesis 16–50* (volumes 1 & 2 in the *Word Bible Commentary* series) by Gordon J. Wenham. Waco, TX: Word Books, 1987, 1994.
- *Genesis 12–50* by A. S. Herbert (Torch Bible Commentaries). London: SCM Press, 1962.
- *Genesis* by Derek Kidner (*Tyndale Old Testament Commentaries*). Downers Grove, IL: InterVarsity Press, 1967.

Most exciting of all, I have included a sample spiritual autobiography, written by my daughter, Jennifer Howe Peace. Jenny was a student in my "Pursuit of Wholeness" class and had first-hand experience in this process. At the beginning of her Ph.D. studies at the Graduate Theological Union in Berkeley, California, she took a course entitled "Symbol and Ritual" taught by Dr. Clare Fischer. Her final paper was entitled "The Role of Journals in My Spiritual Pilgrimage." In it, Jennifer reflected on the themes in the title and illustrated this by telling portions of her own spiritual autobiography. As you will see, she is a talented writer and a deeply perceptive pilgrim. It is exciting to share the writing of this study guide with my daughter. This is the first of what I hope will be other collaborations.

May God bless you as you engage in the task of crafting your spiritual autobiography. To write and to share your story is to grow in who you are. It is to remember that you are part of a great and glorious company who are called the people of God. It is to walk in the way that leads to conformity with the image of Jesus, and to find the wholeness and purpose God intends for us.

The Study Guide at a Glance

What's it all about?
▶ This is a small group program in which each person prepares a spiritual autobiography and then shares it with the small group.
▶ Each person is given a small group session to share and discuss their spiritual autobiography.
▶ This small group study guide is designed to teach you how to construct and share a spiritual autobiography.

What will I learn?
▶ How to examine your life in order to understand some of the ways God has been active in your life.
▶ How to share with others what God has been doing in your life, along with your response to God's activity: the good, the bad, and the ugly!
▶ How to notice the activity of God in your life and in the lives of others (the spiritual discipline of noticing).

How is this study guide put together?
▶ There are three major parts to this study guide:
  • A Small Group Guide with material that will help in the formation of the group and in the study of Abraham's pilgrimage. These small group sessions are undertaken while individual members work on their spiritual autobiographies. You will also find a guide for conducting a spiritual autobiography session in this section.
  • Writing a Spiritual Autobiography: a guide to developing your spiritual autobiography.
  • A Spiritual Autobiography: an example of one person's story.

How does sharing a spiritual autobiography benefit me?
▶ It causes you to notice and to remember what God has been doing in your life over time.
▶ It helps you understand your particular story: who you are, what God has done in and through you, and where God is urging you to go in your pilgrimage.
▶ By sharing your story with others, you (and they) as you come to a better understanding of your uniqueness as a child of God.

Is this course designed for church people only?
▶ No—anyone can join. God is active in everyone's life whether they acknowledge it or not. By joining this group, people who are not consciously following God may be helped to see and understand God's activity in their lives and may respond to God in new ways.
▶ The material in the study guide is written in "ordinary" language for the most part. When theological terms are used, they are explained.

How long will the small group last?

▶ This depends upon the group. You will need at least one formation session, one concluding session, plus a number of sessions equal to the number of people in the group (each person has his or her own session to share their spiritual autobiography).

▶ There are also five Bible studies which focus on the story of Abraham. These can be used by the group while members are preparing their spiritual autobiographies.

What kind of commitment is involved?

▶ Each person must agree to prepare and share a spiritual autobiography.

▶ Each person must agree to abide by the small group covenant which is discussed in the second small group session (page 20).

Will we do Bible Study?

▶ Yes, if you wish. There are five studies from the books of Hebrews and Genesis which focus on the pilgrimage of Abraham. During the weeks when the small group does these Bible studies together, individual members are preparing their spiritual autobiographies. However, it is not necessary to do the Bible studies. After the organizational meeting, you can launch right into the first spiritual autobiography if people are prepared.

How do I recruit members?

▶ All it takes to start a group is the willingness of one person to make some phone calls. When you invite people to join the small group, be sure to explain how the group will operate, since this is a different type of small group. Loan a copy of this book if someone wants a clearer sense of what this group is all about.

The Role of a Spiritual Autobiography

* A spiritual autobiography is the story of God's interaction in our lives. It is a chronicle of our pilgrimage as we seek to follow after God.

* The first spiritual autobiography to be printed was written by Saint Augustine at the end of the fourth century A.D. *The Confessions of Saint Augustine* is a classic of spiritual writing that has influenced countless individuals down through the ages. The title, *Confessions,* has the double meaning of confession as praise to God and confession of one's faults to others. In the *Confessions* Augustine describes how God rescued him from his wayward life and false beliefs. He chronicles both the high points in his interaction with God (e.g., his conversion; the mystical experience he shared with this mother Monica) and the low points in his life (his taking of a mistress and later sending her away; his hedonistic lifestyle). But in all of the ups and downs of his life, the reader detects a note of astonishment on the part of Augustine. He is amazed that God in his grace rescued him from his errant ideas and self-destructive behavior.[1]

Many other spiritual autobiographies have been written since Augustine's groundbreaking effort. In the seventeenth century, the Puritans wrote spiritual autobiographies, stimulated by their need to give a personal testimony in order to become members of the church. Recently, spiritual autobiography has become a major genre in Christian literature. For example, hundreds of thousands of people on both sides of the Atlantic have read about C. S. Lewis' journey to faith in *Surprised by Joy.* They have read about his ongoing pilgrimage in the scores of letters Lewis wrote to correspondents around the world (e.g., *Letters to an American Lady*). Then there is Thomas Merton's *Seven Storey Mountain* in which he tells of his pilgrimage from being a cynical intellectual to becoming a Trappist monk. Merton has helped many to understand the monastic life. Dan Wakefield, screenwriter and author, tells the story of his spiritual journey in *Returning.* He subsequently wrote *The Story of Your Life: Writing a Spiritual Autobiography* in which he helps others in this process. Spiritual autobiography has become a significant form of spiritual exploration.

Spiritual autobiography is not limited to great saints and their extraordinary
* deeds nor to literary giants who can write with clarity and force. We all have the ability to write a spiritual autobiography. In fact, each person has a story to tell. Every one of us could write a spiritual autobiography because God is active in each of our lives. Now to be sure, persistent refusal to hear and heed that Voice reduces it to a mere whisper and relegates it to the background of many lives. And more than a few people would be surprised to hear that they have anything to write about God. And yet when considered, there are hints of the divine in all lives: long-forgotten childhood experiences of God's presence; answers to prayer that were quickly shrugged off as "coincidence"; grace in the midst of pain; moments of joy that rush in unexpectedly; responses to nature that draw us outward; deep suspicion that maybe our mechanistic "explanations" to the way the universe operates are not quite as sound as we
* would like them to be; encounters with powers that are quite beyond us; wor-

ship that we did not initiate and could not contain; a sense of blessing that gives us hope and direction; a knowledge that somehow we are significant in this world. God is alive and active in his universe and when we start to notice, it is hard to stop the process.

This is one reason why it is so useful to write a spiritual autobiography. It puts us in touch with the way things really are in life and draws us toward the true meaning of life; it reveals unnoticed but foundational aspects of our lives; it draws the strands of our lives together in a creative way that points us to the purpose and meaning of our lives; it reminds us of where true reality lies over against the illusions of modern life. In a sentence, a spiritual autobiography encourages us to notice God and, in noticing, our lives are changed.

The process of writing a spiritual autobiography is not difficult. It simply takes a little time, the willingness to explore areas we have previously left unexamined, and a hungry curiosity about God. Writing a spiritual autobiography is best done in the company of others who are engaged in the same task. We motivate each other to continue with the exploration; we encourage each other when the writing slows down; and most importantly, we are there to hear the finished work because the telling of our tale is very important.

Spiritual Autobiography and Ordinary Autobiography

One issue you will face is how to sort out the "spiritual" dimensions of your life from all of the other dimensions. In the absolute sense, of course, this is not possible. Life does not fit into neat categories, nor does God operate only in a carefully prescribed realm. In fact, God is present in all aspects of life: in the ordinary acts of eating ("Give us this day our daily bread"), sleeping (the people in the Bible knew that God could and did speak through "night visions"), and making love (God is the one who gave us our sexual natures). God is found in events, in our choices, and, especially, in our relationships. It is often through the "ordinary" that we encounter the "extraordinary." It is out of the mundane, everyday stuff of life that we forge our understanding of the spiritual. God's presence is written in nature, in our musings, and in the routine activities that take up so much of our time. God is everywhere. So a spiritual autobiography is not easily disentangled from the rest of our story, nor is it intended to be.

But after having said this, I also need to say that there is a spiritual dimension to life and that it is possible to identify this. What distinguishes a spiritual autobiography from an ordinary autobiography is the lens through which we look at our lives. In this case, we view our lives through the lens of the spiritual and search for God's footprints in our unfolding lives. We focus on the aspects that reveal to us the activity of God. What distinguishes a spiritual autobiography from ordinary autobiography is the search for the presence of God.

A traditional autobiography tells the story of a life in sequential order, including all of the "facts" that make that story unique. But the writer must select some information to include and some to leave out. Who could possibly record a whole life? Who could possibly read such an account? No, a tale is told for a reason: to justify a life; to track the development of genius; to account for a life lived for good or ill; to boast; to explain; to understand. A spiritual autobiography, on the other hand, is told in order to see the activity of God.

But here is the rub. Most of the time we don't notice the spiritual. God is like the air we breathe. We merely assume God, just as we assume air. So this is the challenge in a spiritual autobiography: to notice God. This defines the nature of the hunt: to know God in as many ways as we can. We dare not simply say: "God is everywhere" (which is true) and then claim, "So what more can I say?" (which is a cop-out). We must start by identifying those seminal points when we have been aware of God. These may be major events (the birth of a child, a wedding, a funeral, a conversion) or hints of transcendence (the joy of a sunset, being moved by music or poetry, being struck by a passage of Scripture that helps make sense out of a problem).

To write a spiritual autobiography is to learn a new way of seeing. It is to bridge the gap between the natural and the spiritual. It is to become newly sensitive to the hidden work of God. It is to live simultaneously in the two worlds we were created to inhabit—the spiritual and the physical—and in the process to become a whole person. This is why spiritual autobiography can be called a spiritual discipline: it is teaching us a new way of seeing; it is bringing the sense of God into the immediacy of life; it is noticing God.

Spiritual Autobiography and Witness

Your spiritual autobiography is not the same as the story of your first encounter with Jesus. In evangelical circles, the giving of witness has often been restricted to sharing the story of one's conversion. Now to be sure, conversion is a central element in our tale. But it is not the only element. We also need to notice and describe the many ways in which we encountered God both prior to and after conversion. To hear some people speak, it is almost as if the only important event in their spiritual lives is conversion. This is a distortion of the New Testament understanding of the Christian life where conversion marks a turning from one way to a new Way. Conversion is the beginning of a crucial new phase of spiritual experience; it is not the end of the story, nor is it the beginning of that story.

Likewise, to equate witness with sharing the story of one's conversion is to limit witness severely. How often does the opportunity present itself to take five to ten minutes to describe your conversion? The answer is: not often, if at all, except in church circles. Since this is the case, much of the so-called training in evangelism consists of learning how to manipulate a situation so that you can "give a testimony." The result in real life is often unnatural and awkward. The one who receives such witness feels awkward and embarrassed. The impact is minimal or negative.

How much better is witness when it arises spontaneously in the context of an ongoing conversation! If we know about the many and varied ways we meet

God, we have much—not simply one thing—to say. In the end, true witness is simply being honest about our ongoing experience of God.

Herein lies the problem. If we are not in touch with the activity of God in our lives, then we cannot talk about it. This is why writing a spiritual autobiography can be such a powerful aid in sharing our faith with those around us who seem oblivious to the supernatural. In writing a spiritual autobiography, we begin to notice God's activity in our lives—in big and in small ways. We connect this activity to specific incidents, which means that we have many little stories that we can share in the course of ordinary conversation. And these kinds of stories are less likely to intimidate our hearers. They whet a person's appetite to explore his or her own life for the presence of God. They raise the right kind of questions such as, "How can I know God? How can I stay connected to God? What is prayer? Where can I learn about who God is?"

Here is a suggestion: how about telling a friend at work that you are in the process of trying to write a spiritual autobiography? See what he or she says. I suspect that you will get into a good conversation about faith issues—which is what witness is all about.

Spiritual Autobiography and Growth

Perhaps the main reason we write a spiritual autobiography is so that we will grow as Christians. This happens in several ways. First, by seeing our stories as a whole we understand at a new level God's intention for us. We understand life's purpose and our calling. We see where we fit in God's scheme of things. All the people of God have a role to play in the kingdom of God, though each person's role is different. Sometimes we can only understand our particular role when we see our lives in their overall context. We see how the pieces fit together. We discern how seemingly unrelated elements combine to prepare us for our various works.

Second, we grow by seeing that God has, indeed, been present and active in our lives. We are too close to the events in our lives as they unfold. We may catch hints of meaning and suspect there is purpose in them. But it is only when we view them through the lens of the whole that we grasp their meaning. And we are encouraged. We find that we do, in fact, have a place in the work of God. We emerge energized to serve God in these ways.

Third, we gain some sense of the direction where our lives are pointing. We discern the trajectories of our history. In understanding the meaning of our past, we understand better the meaning of the present, and glimpse something of what the future might hold. This sense of direction is especially important when we are faced with a decision about the direction of our lives. Should we take the new job? Are we called to seminary? Does God want us to become a small group leader? Or a missionary? Or an accountant? Knowing our past helps us in our decisions about the future. Sensing the meaning of our lives, we can make the choices that are consistent with that past.

Finally, by writing a spiritual autobiography we develop the ability to notice the work of God in our lives. Having seen God at work in the past, we are alert to God's working in the present. And finding God in the present—knowing our lives have meaning, and experiencing what it means to be loved—encourages and energizes us to continue in our pilgrimage.

Sources of Data for a Spiritual Autobiography

Where do you go to find the information necessary to write a spiritual autobiography? I want to suggest several sources:

Memory

Some people only have to ask the right question in order to unlock deep memories. Simply by asking "Where was God when I was a child (teenager, college student, parent, etc.)?" brings to mind all kinds of incidents. I suggest that you begin at this point in working on your spiritual autobiography. Once you have outlined the major periods of your life, explore each period in the ways recommended in the following chapters. Begin with the period that is most alive and vivid to you. Try to recall what it was like. Take notes. Be alert to thoughts that strike you or incidents that you suddenly recall. Work through each of the periods in your life in this way.

Conversation

Significant events in your spiritual life may well have taken place in the presence of others. Or you may have recounted an event to friends or family members. Sometimes they have a better recollection of what went on than you. Or they may recall details that you have forgotten. It is certainly worth some phone calls to see if this is the case.

Every family has its historian. They may not know that this is their role, but the fact is that they know more than anyone else about the history of the family. They know the stories. They remember what happened, who is related to whom, why one cousin no longer talks to another, who was at a family wedding twenty years ago, what the religious history of the family is, where the family skeletons are locked away, etc. You may need to talk to the historian in your family. Again, it is worth a phone call or a lunch. Bring such a person into your project. He or she will love to help.

Journals

The first book in the SPIRITUAL DISCIPLINES series is about spiritual journaling. It describes one way of assembling data in order to write a spiritual autobiography. This is what the Puritans did. They kept journals, which they considered the daily record of their sacred journey. From those journals they came to understand the story of their pilgrimage. If you have kept a journal for any length of time, reading over your journal is the best way to get material for a spiritual autobiography. See, for example, the spiritual autobiography in Part III of this book. It is based on a set of fifteen journals.

However, keeping a journal is one thing; writing a spiritual autobiography is another. In the simplest terms, a journal is the raw data from which a spiritual autobiography can be constructed. In a journal we write down the pieces of our lives: the everyday events and feelings; our reflections and impressions about life as it unfolds before us. Journals are of special value in writing a spiritual autobiography when we have used our journals to assess and understand past periods of our lives.[2] We process our history by going back and examining our lives through a grid that includes such things as our key relationships, principal activities, important ideas, physical experiences, and spiritual encounters. The point is that in each period of our lives, we can find the footprints of God in the context of the issues that define that period of time.

Prayer

In the end it is the Holy Spirit who reveals what we need to know in order to piece together a spiritual autobiography. We need to be clear about this. We need to pray for light. We must ask the Spirit to show us what we need to know about our lives in order to understand them from a spiritual point of view.

And then we need to listen. The Holy Spirit will lead us in various ways. Sometimes it is through our memory. If an incident pops into your head, do not dismiss it quickly. Think about it. Write it down. At other times it is through our awareness and observation. After asking for guidance, we are alert to guidance. So a chance remark by a friend, a phrase in a book, an incident in a TV show, a story in the Bible, a prayer we are reading, a dream—whatever—sparks a new line of inquiry.

Writing a spiritual autobiography is as much a matter of memory as anything. We don't remember our entire life, but we recall the seminal, defining incidents. At the time, the importance of the situation may not have struck us. But in retrospect, we see the significance of what went on. We need the Holy Spirit to guide us to such crucial incidents. And if we ask, we will be guided.

---

[1]How to speak about God is a problem. The Bible generally uses masculine language (and occasionally feminine terms)—not, of course, to imply gender but to indicate personhood. An increasing number of Christians are offended by strict masculine language (knowing the God of the Bible is not male nor female). Others are offended by gender-neutral language. I have chosen to use traditional masculine pronouns on those occasions when they are required, but I recognize that God is not male and that the English language is deficient at this point.

[2]See the first book in the SPIRITUAL DISCIPLINES series: *Spiritual Journaling: Recording Your Journey Toward God* by Richard Peace (NavPress, 1995) in which a method of journaling is described that helps individuals to assess their past.

PART I—SMALL GROUP SESSIONS: THE PILGRIMAGE OF ABRAHAM

Pilgrimage

Preparing for Sharing: To write a spiritual autobiography is a sacred task: sacred in that the process makes us aware of the spiritual dimensions of our lives. It is God's nature to be active in all lives at all times. But not all people notice—much less respond to—God. To write a spiritual autobiography is to notice, and noticing enables us to respond in new ways to God. In this session you will discuss the process of preparing a spiritual autobiography.

Bible Study Theme: Our spiritual autobiography is the story of our pilgrimage. The model for pilgrimage is Abraham. It was out of his obedience that the nation of Israel was formed and from which the Christian church emerged. In studying Abraham's story you will gain valuable insight about the form of a pilgrimage.

Session Aims: The purpose of this first session is to:
- begin the process of group-building by sharing some of your stories with one another;
- discuss the process of writing a spiritual autobiography;
- do a Bible study that introduces the idea of pilgrimage and introduces Abraham's pilgrimage (Hebrews 11:1–3,8–10; 12:1–2).

Stories (20 minutes)

At the beginning of each session you will be asked to share a mini-story: an incident from your life that connects with the theme of this session.

Biographies

The story of your life is a network of intersecting stories: the story of your family; the story of your community and schools; the story of your friends and acquaintances—and how all this, along with your own internal story, have made you who you are.

1. Introduce yourself to the group:
   - Briefly describe one fact about yourself that others in the group might not have guessed (e.g., you grow prize-winning lilies; your hobby is bass fishing; you once met a famous person).
   - Give one reason why you came to this small group.

2. Take a few minutes to identify the <u>important people</u> in your story:

✓✓ ☑ your parents   ❏ your siblings
     ❏ your relatives   ❏ your heroes/heroines
     ❏ your spouse and children   ❏ your important friends
     ❏ your mentors   .   *✓✓ grandmother*
✓ *✓ mother as chief*

3. When were you first aware of God's entrance into your story? Explain.

Discuss (15/20 minutes)

Writing a Spiritual Autobiography

Review the material on pages 9–14 and then discuss the process of preparing a spiritual autobiography.

1. As you think about writing a spiritual autobiography:
   - What is the most exciting aspect of this process for you?
   - What is the most frightening aspect of this process for you?

2. How will you gather data for your spiritual autobiography?
   ❏ from journals   ❏ from parents
   ❏ from relatives   ❏ from photo albums
   ❏ from memory   ❏ from telephone conversations
   ❏ from reading   ❏ from other sources: _____

3. What motivates you the most in this spiritual autobiography project?
   ❏ the chance to explore God's actions in my life
   ❏ the desire to be more self-aware
   ❏ the need to know what next steps God wants me to take
   ❏ the desire to track God's impact on my life
   ❏ the wish to understand more about the meaning of my life
   ❏ the chance to make sense of my past
   ❏ the desire to notice the presence of God
   ❏ the need to know my growing edge
   ❏ a hungry curiosity
   ❏ other: _____

Study (20/40 minutes)

The Christian pilgrimage is characterized by two features: movement and goal. Specifically, Christians are persons who press on in their spiritual lives (they try not to get stalled, side-tracked, or trapped in one place). And they have a clear sense of their goal (to be conformed to the image of Christ). Faith is the energy that drives their pilgrimage forward. In chapters 11 and 12 of Hebrews, the author describes both the process (goal-oriented pilgrimage) and the energy (God-given faith) of pilgrimage. Read over these excerpts and the Bible study notes on page 90:

Hebrews 11

Now faith is being sure of what we hope for and certain of what we do not see. This is what the ancients were commended for. By faith we understand that the universe was formed at God's command, so that what is seen was not made out of what was visible. . . .

By faith Abraham, when called to go to a place he would later receive as his inheritance, obeyed and went, even though he did not know where he was going. By faith he made his home in the promised land like a stranger in a foreign country; he lived in tents, as did Isaac and Jacob, who were heirs with him of the same promise. For he was looking forward to the city with foundations, whose architect and builder is God. . . .

Hebrews 12

Therefore, since we are surrounded by such a great cloud of witnesses, let us throw off everything that hinders and the sin that so easily entangles, and let us run with perseverance the race marked out for us. Let us fix our eyes on Jesus, the author and perfecter of our faith, who for the joy set before him endured the cross, scorning its shame, and sat down at the right hand of the throne of God.

1. The function of faith:
   - In Hebrews 11:3, the author gives one example of how faith operates in everyday life. What is his example and how does it illustrate faith in operation?
   - How does faith function in your relationships? in your spiritual life? in your understanding of the future?
   - In what ways does faith energize a pilgrim's journey?

2. Abraham's faith:
   - In what ways did Abraham demonstrate his faith in God?
   - What was the nature of his movement? What was his goal? How did faith play a part in his life?

3. Pilgrimage: Abraham is one of the witnesses that the writer of Hebrews points to in Chapters 11 and 12. On the basis of their experience:
   - What hinders a person's pilgrimage?
   - How ought a person conduct his or her pilgrimage?
   - In what ways is Jesus a pilgrim's example? What was the goal toward which he pressed?

4. Our pilgrimage: What do you learn for your pilgrimage from this passage:
   - About movement/process?
   - About goal/outcome?
   - About the role of faith?

Optional: Discuss the following statement: "To be a pilgrim demands a kind of holy restlessness that keeps us moving, and a kind of invigorating hope that keeps us focused."

Pray (5/10 minutes)

End your time with prayer together in a manner which is appropriate to your group. Pray about:

- the formation of the group: that the people in this small group will be drawn together and begin to feel a connection with one another.
- the writing of spiritual autobiographies: that each person will find the desire and the will to engage in this process; that in so doing, new insight will emerge; and that the process itself will be energizing.
- understanding the nature and meaning of pilgrimage: from a personal point of view.
- openness to God: that each person will know God in new ways.

Homework

Read over "The Role of a Spiritual Autobiography" and Part II of this workbook to get an idea of how to write a spiritual autobiography. Also read Part III for an example of what a spiritual autobiography might look like. As thoughts occur to you about your spiritual journey, make notes. This will help you later when you actually put together your spiritual autobiography.

Call and Blessing

Preparing for Sharing: In order to feel comfortable sharing your life with others, you need to be clear about the character of the group. What is expected of each person? Will what you share be kept confidential? How will the group function? These questions are covered in a group covenant. A covenant makes explicit the ground rules of the group. In this session you will decide on a covenant together.

Bible Study Theme: Abraham's pilgrimage begins with a call and blessing from God to leave his country, clan, and family home and go to Canaan, an unknown land. We also need to hear God's call and receive his blessing on our pilgrimages.

Session Aims: The purpose of this second session is to:
- continue the process of group-building by sharing more of your stories with one another;
- commit to a covenant to guide your small group sharing;
- do a Bible study on Abraham's call and blessing by God as Abraham begins his pilgrimage to the promised land (Genesis 12:1–5).

Stories (20 minutes)

Family Stories

We learn the meaning of our own story as we hear the stories of our family, community, faith tradition, and nation.

1. When is your family most likely to tell family stories?
   - ☒ at holiday gatherings
   - ☐ during summer vacations
   - ☐ by long distance phone calls
   - ☒ at large family dinners/picnics
   - ☒ when siblings get together
   - ☐ at weddings (baptisms; confirmations)
   - ☐ in letters
   - ☒ around the campfire
   - ☐ in everyday gossip
   - ☐ never
   - ☐ other: _____

2. Tell a favorite family story about one of the following:
   - ☐ a family trip
   - ☐ an unusual friend or relative
   - ☐ a prank
   - ☒ a summer vacation
   - ☐ a TV show or movie
   - ☐ a sports event
   - ☐ a habit or idiosyncrasy
   - ☐ an embarrassing moment
   - ☐ any other event

3. How did Christianity enter into your family history, if at all? Who is the most religious person in your extended family? The least religious?

Discuss (15/20 minutes)
Creating a Covenant

Every small group needs a covenant (or contract) that defines how the group will function. A covenant is a set of ground rules that guide interaction and establish expectations. What follows is a draft of a covenant for your Spiritual Autobiography Small Group. Adapt it to your group by answering the following questions:

- Should any of the ground rules be deleted?
- Should any new items be added?

When you are all agreed, sign your covenant, pray together and offer this covenant to God.

Small Group Covenant

- **Attendance:** I agree to be at the session each week unless a genuine emergency arises.

- **Participation:** I will enter enthusiastically into group discussion and sharing.

- **Confidentiality:** I will not share with anyone outside the group the stories of those in the group.

- **Honesty:** I will be forthright and truthful in what is said: if I do not feel I can share something, I will say "I pass" for that question.

- **Openness:** I will be candid with others in appropriate ways and allow others to share for themselves.

- **Respect:** I will not judge others, give advice, or criticize.

- **Care:** I will be open to the needs of others in appropriate ways.

Signed: _____

Study (20/40 minutes)

Abraham is the father of the Jewish nation. As such, he is an important figure not only to Jews but also to Christians and Muslims. This makes him one of the most important men in the history of the world. What makes Abraham so important to so many people is not his sterling character (which he did not have), his outstanding intellect (which may have existed but it is not mentioned), his charming personality (he could be pretty annoying) or substantial personal accomplishments (he has few, apart from his pilgrimage to the promised land). What Abraham is remembered for is his faithfulness in obeying God's call to undertake a long and demanding journey. It was not so much what Abraham did as what *God* did.

Abraham's pilgrimage is a model for our pilgrimages. Not that we will experience exactly what Abraham experienced. It is a model in that it defines the ways in which God interacts in human lives. Abraham's pilgrimage contains many of the elements common to pilgrimages: success, failure, faithfulness, unfaithfulness, troubled relationships, fulfilling relationships, etc. In other words, in Abraham we see an ordinary man who is used by God, not because of who Abraham was, but because of who God is. It also says something very important about God. It is possible to have a relationship with God. It is God who calls people. It is God who uses people to accomplish His tasks.

It was Paul who said: "Consider Abraham" in his letter to the Galatians (3:6). In other words, "Learn from him." This is what we propose to do. In learning about Abraham we learn about ourselves; specifically, we gain insight about the anatomy of a pilgrimage. This is important since our spiritual autobiography is the story of our pilgrimage.

Genesis 12

The LORD had said to Abram, "Leave your country, your people and your father's household and go to the land I will show you.

"I will make you into a great nation and I will bless you; I will make your name great, and you will be a blessing.

"I will bless those who bless you, and whoever curses you I will curse; and all peoples on earth will be blessed through you."

So Abram left, as the LORD had told him; and Lot went with him. Abram was seventy-five years old when he set out from Haran. He took his wife Sarai, his nephew Lot, all the possessions they had accumulated and the people they had acquired in Haran, and they set out for the land of Canaan, and they arrived there.

1. Abraham's call:
   • What is the command God gives to Abraham?
   • What price must Abraham pay in order to obey this call?

2. God's promise:
   • What does God promise Abraham directly and by implication?
   • What does it mean to be blessed by God? to bless others?

3. Abraham's obedience:
   • What difficulties must Abraham have experienced in obeying God's call?
   • What made it possible for him to overcome these difficulties?

4. Your call:
   • In the past, what has God called you to do or be?
   • Now what is God asking of you?
     ❏ a new obedience   ❏ a new task
     ❏ a new ministry   ❏ a new faithfulness
     ❏ a new step   ❏ a change of heart
     ❏ nothing   ❏ I don't know

- What is the price of obedience to this calling?
- In what ways are you being called to "leave home"? Why?

5. Your blessing:
   - If to be blessed is to be affirmed and empowered for the future, who has played this role in your life? How?

☐ a grandparent   ☐ a parent
☒ a spouse   ☐ a sibling
☒ a wise friend/counselor   ☐ yourself
☐ no one   ☐ other: _____
☐ a teacher

- Whom have you blessed or could you bless? What would this mean to them?

Optional: Discuss the following statement: "To hear God's call assumes we have learned to hear God; to obey God's command assumes we have learned what it means to obey God."

Pray (5/10 minutes)

End your time with prayer together in a manner which is appropriate to your group. Pray about:
- the formation of the group: that you will grow to love and trust one another; that you will become the kind of friends that support one another;
- the presentation of your stories: that each will grow and learn from the stories; that in the telling, each person will grow more certain of his or her identify in Christ;
- the covenant: that God will use this to bind you together and to guide your deliberations;
- the call and blessing: that each person will hear God's call and be given the grace to respond in positive ways; that the hardships that stand in the way of obedience will be overcome; that each person will be blessed and give blessings.

Homework

Finish reading Parts II and III of this workbook. This week work on defining the major periods in your spiritual journey (see pages 41–45). This work will give you a time structure in which to tell your story.

Encounters

Preparing for Sharing: While there is great value in writing a spiritual auto-biography, there is even more value in sharing it. This is because:

- in the telling of our story, we come to accept who we are in new ways.
- in the hearing of other's stories, we come to understand better our own stories.
- in the telling and the hearing, we are bound together in new and deep ways with those in our group, and, by extension, with all of God's people.

In this session you will discuss the process of sharing spiritual autobiographies.

Bible Study Theme: Abraham has been on his pilgrimage now for a number of years. It has not been easy. He has dealt with strife in his family, with war, and with famine. Furthermore, God has not yet fulfilled his promise to give Abraham an heir from whom a great nation will arise. In the passage you will study, God speaks to Abraham once again, this time in mystical ways. In our pilgrimages, it is often the unusual, the unexpected, the deep encounter that sheds new light on our paths and gives us renewed energy to continue the journey.

Session Aims: The purpose of this third session is to:

- continue the process of group-building;
- discuss the process of sharing a spiritual autobiography;
- create a schedule for sharing;
- do a Bible study on Abraham's mystical encounter with God (Genesis 15:1–21)

Stories (20 minutes)

Strange Happenings

God speaks to us in various ways: sometimes softly, sometimes loudly, most often indirectly. What we are discussing today are the experiences of "presence" which are rare for most people, but which are deep in meaning and clearly have the sense of divine about them.

1. In which of the following experiences or environments have you experienced the presence of God (or the supernatural) in an unusual way? Check all that apply:

❑ a mystical experience   ❑ a conversion experience
❑ a dream with deep meaning   ❑ reading a Bible passage
❑ an unusual worship experience   ❑ in nature
❑ in a time of prayer   ❑ in music or art
❑ the still, small inner "voice"   ❑ through an event
❑ in a relationship   ❑ by means of inconsolable longing
❑ in conversation   ❑ during childbirth or lovemaking
❑ through a "coincidence" (which is really God acting)
❑ in an encounter with a child or a wise person

2. Share briefly one of these experiences. (Remember that you may cover this in more detail when you present your spiritual autobiography.)

3. If you could ask God for one type of encounter with him right now, what would it be? What do you want most from God?

Discuss (15/20 minutes)

Sharing a Spiritual Autobiography

Review the material in Session Six (pages 35–37) and then discuss the process of presenting a spiritual autobiography.

1. As you think about presenting a spiritual autobiography:
   - What is the most exciting aspect of this process for you?
   - What is the most frightening aspect of this process for you?
   - What will help you most when it is your turn to present?

2. Together, produce a schedule for sharing spiritual autobiographies. Who will share on which date? Include in your schedule the name of the person who will lead the post-presentation discussion.

Study (20/40 minutes)

The issue in this chapter is barrenness. The response is a renewed promise and a new covenant from God. At the heart of this story is a complex encounter with God that has several parts to it. First there is a vision. Then there is deep sleep and God's presence passes through the sacrifice. In this story various issues are raised: the nature of God's promises, the delay in fulfillment, and how faith and encounters with God function in our lives. In this story Abraham is seen as prophet, priest, and king. As with other prophets he is granted a vision (verse 1) and a prophecy about the future (verses 13–16). As priest he prepares and offers a sacrifice to God (verses 9–11). As king, he is promised a land and victory over his foes (verses 16, 18–21).

Genesis 15

After this, the word of the LORD came to Abram in a vision:
> "Do not be afraid, Abram.
> I am your shield,
> your very great reward."

But Abram said, "O Sovereign LORD, what can you give me since I remain childless and the one who will inherit my estate is Eliezer of Damascus?" And Abram said, "You have given me no children; so a servant in my household will be my heir."
Then the word of the LORD came to him: "This man will not be your heir, but a son coming from your own body will be your heir." He took him outside and said, "Look up at the heavens and count the stars —if indeed you can count them." Then he said to him, "So shall your offspring be."
Abram believed the LORD, and he credited it to him as righteousness.

He also said to him, "I am the LORD, who brought you out of Ur of the Chaldeans to give you this land to take possession of it."

But Abram said, "O Sovereign LORD, how can I know that I will gain possession of it?"

So the LORD said to him, "Bring me a heifer, a goat and a ram, each three years old, along with a dove and a young pigeon."

Abram brought all these to him, cut them in two and arranged the halves opposite each other; the birds, however, he did not cut in half. Then birds of prey came down on the carcasses, but Abram drove them away.

As the sun was setting, Abram fell into a deep sleep, and a thick and dreadful darkness came over him. Then the LORD said to him, "Know for certain that your descendants will be strangers in a country not their own, and they will be enslaved and mistreated four hundred years. But I will punish the nation they serve as slaves, and afterward they will come out with great possessions. You, however, will go to your fathers in peace and be buried at a good old age. In the fourth generation your descendants will come back here, for the sin of the Amorites has not yet reached its full measure."

When the sun had set and darkness had fallen, a smoking firepot with a blazing torch appeared and passed between the pieces. On that day the LORD made a covenant with Abram and said, "To your descendants I give this land, from the river of Egypt to the great river, the Euphrates—the land of the Kenites, Kenizzites, Kadmonites, Hittites, Perizzites, Rephaites, Amorites, Canaanites, Girgashites and Jebusites."

1. The promise:
   • Review the list in question 1 of the *Stories* exercise. In how many ways does God reveal himself here to Abraham?
   • What are the three promises given to Abraham in this chapter (verses 1, 4–5, 18–21)?
   • What prophecy is given to Abraham (verses 13–16)?

2. The protest:
   • What is Abraham's first protest (verses 2–3)? Why does Abraham protest?
   • How does Abraham respond to God's word and sign?
   • What is Abraham's second protest (verse 8)?

3. The response:
   • What moved Abraham from protest in verses 2–3 to faith in (verse 6?
   • How does God respond to his second inquiry?
   • What is the connection between faith and delay? Between faith and encounter with God?

4. Encounters: It is one thing to have a mystical experience with God; it is another to live in God's presence daily:
   • In what ways do you know God's presence in daily life?

5. Problems: It is one thing to know God's promises and presence; it is another to live with the doubts, issues, and delays that comprise the walk of faith for most people.
   • What have been (or are) your complaints to God?
   • What role, if any, has doubt played in your pilgrimage?
   • How do you deal with the delays (the time gap between promise and fulfillment; between prayer and response)?

Optional: Discuss the following statement: "To open ourselves to the supernatural is a tricky business. We need to be sure it is God whom we have met, and we need to be sure that our experience is not just wishful thinking."

Pray (5/10 minutes)

End your time with prayer together in a manner which is appropriate to your group. Pray about:

- the writing of the spiritual autobiography: that each person will be able to do what is necessary;
- the whole experience of sharing a spiritual autobiography: that nervousness may be overcome, that it will be a powerful and positive experience for both presenter and group;
- the encounter with God: that each person will understand how we meet God; that there will be openness to God's presence;
- the role of faith in our lives: that each person's faith will be strengthened; that we will be able to deal with the delays, the doubts, and the questions raised in our pilgrimages; that it will be said of us that we believed God and that it was credited as righteousness to us.

Homework

Now that you know when your spiritual autobiography is due, develop a schedule so you will be finished in plenty of time. Start working on the phase of your story which is clearest to you. It is important to begin writing your story or making notes to guide your telling of it. Beginning is always the hardest step.

Relationships

Preparing for Sharing: By now group members have begun work on their spiritual autobiographies. We need encouragement from one another in this process. For some, writing a spiritual autobiography is an easy task; for others it is difficult. A few people find it an almost impossible assignment. In this session you will check in with each other about your progress and then encourage each other to finish your preparation.

Bible Study Theme: It is easy to idealize Abraham. But Abraham is far from perfect. And lest we be intimidated (believing that he is so far beyond us that he is not a model for poor, weak folk like us), the two incidents you will study are reminders of his fallibility. As we seek to understand our pilgrimages we realize that our stories are not simply stories of great success. They are also stories of failure. Both success and failure are vital parts of our tale. We also learn that our failures are often found in our relationships.

Session Aims: The purpose of this fourth session is to:
- report on how we are doing in preparing a spiritual autobiography;
- reflect on our relationships in our pilgrimage;
- do a Bible study on Abraham's relationships with various people (Genesis 16:1–6; 20:1–15).

Stories (20 minutes)

Friends and Relatives

At the heart of our lives are our friends and relatives.

1. When you were a child, who were the three most important people in your world? What was the best thing you remember about these relationships?
   ❐ grandparents ❐ parents
   ❐ siblings ❐ relatives (aunts, cousins, etc.)
   ❐ neighborhood friends ❐ vacation friends
   ❐ imaginary friends ❐ pets
   ❐ others: _____

2. When you were a teenager, who was your best friend? Describe him or her and explain why you were such good friends.

3. Have you ever had a "spiritual friendship"; i.e., a relationship that centered on your pursuit of God? If so, describe it. If not, what do you think such a friendship would be like?

Discuss (15/20 minutes)

Working on a Spiritual Autobiography

At this point most people in the group are immersed in the process of preparing their spiritual autobiography. Use this discussion time to give progress reports.

1. Where are you in the process of preparing your spiritual autobiography:
   - ❐ All done
   - ❐ In the midst of it
   - ❐ I work best under pressure
   - ❐ Almost done
   - ❐ Just getting started
   - ❐ Was I supposed to be working on that?

2. First pick the easiest part of the process for you and then review the list and identify the hardest part:
   - ❐ getting started
   - ❐ remembering
   - ❐ getting information
   - ❐ knowing what to do
   - ❐ dealing with doubts and fears
   - ❐ writing it down
   - ❐ finding time
   - ❐ overcoming roadblocks
   - ❐ getting motivated
   - ❐ other: _____

3. How can the group pray for you as you work on your spiritual autobiography?

Study (20/40 minutes)

It is easy enough to think of a person like Abraham as some sort of saint: a man graced by the presence of God who lives each step of his life in a righteous, godly sort of way. After all, look at who he is: the father of a great nation, revered by the people of three of the world's great religions. Look at what he experienced: the direct presence of God, not once but on several occasions, calling him to a momentous task. Look at what he did: he believed God and so became the model for salvation; he followed God and so became the model for pilgrimage. But while all of this is true, it does not fully describe Abraham. He is a mix of faithfulness and fault; a man who gets it right some of the time and wrong at other times. In fact, in Abraham we see not so much a saint in action; rather, the faithfulness and graciousness of God.

We are going to look at two incidents in the Abraham's life, both dealing with relationships, both involving a relational triangle. In the first, Sarah decides to solve the problem of her barrenness in her own way. It doesn't work. In the second incident, Abraham deals with another problem: his fear. He is no wiser than Sarah and also gets into trouble. In these two incidents we see that pilgrimage is no panacea; we do stupid things along the way that mess up our relationships, and this too is part of our stories. It is what we must confront in knowing ourselves and knowing God's work in our lives.

Genesis 16

Now Sarai, Abram's wife, had borne him no children. But she had an Egyptian maidservant named Hagar; so she said to Abram, "The LORD has kept me from having children. Go, sleep with my maidservant; perhaps I can build a family through her."

Abram agreed to what Sarai said. So after Abram had been living in Canaan ten years, Sarai his wife took her Egyptian maidservant Hagar and gave her to her husband to be his wife. He slept with Hagar, and she conceived.

When she knew she was pregnant, she began to despise her mistress. Then Sarai said to Abram, "You are responsible for the wrong I am suffering. I put my servant in your arms, and now that she knows she is pregnant, she despises me. May the LORD judge between you and me."

"Your servant is in your hands," Abram said. "Do with her whatever you think best." Then Sarai mistreated Hagar; so she fled from her. . . .

Genesis 20

Now Abraham moved on from there into the region of the Negev and lived between Kadesh and Shur. For a while he stayed in Gerar, and there Abraham said of his wife Sarah, "She is my sister." Then Abimelech king of Gerar sent for Sarah and took her.

But God came to Abimelech in a dream one night and said to him, "You are as good as dead because of the woman you have taken; she is a married woman."

Now Abimelech had not gone near her, so he said, "Lord, will you destroy an innocent nation? Did he not say to me, 'She is my sister,' and didn't she also say, 'He is my brother'? I have done this with a clear conscience and clean hands."

Then God said to him in the dream, "Yes, I know you did this with a clear conscience, and so I have kept you from sinning against me. That is why I did not let you touch her. Now return the man's wife, for he is a prophet, and he will pray for you and you will live. But if you do not return her, you may be sure that you and all yours will die."

Early the next morning Abimelech summoned all his officials, and when he told them all that had happened, they were very much afraid. Then Abimelech called Abraham in and said, "What have you done to us? How have I wronged you that you have brought such great guilt upon me and my kingdom? You have done things to me that should not be done." And Abimelech asked Abraham, "What was your reason for doing this?"

Abraham replied, "I said to myself, 'There is surely no fear of God in this place, and they will kill me because of my wife.' Besides, she really is my sister, the daughter of my father though not of my mother; and she became my wife. And when God had me wander from my father's household, I said to her, 'This is how you can show your love to me: Everywhere we go, say of me, 'He is my brother.' ' "

Then Abimelech brought sheep and cattle and male and female slaves and gave them to Abraham, and he returned Sarah his wife to him.

And Abimelech said, "My land is before you; live wherever you like."

1. Issues:
   - What is the problem in the first story, and how does Sarah propose to solve it?
   - How would you define and assess Abraham's role in all of this?
   - What was the outcome of this first venture: Who was hurt and how?
   - What is the problem in the second story, and how does Abraham propose to solve it?
   - How would you define and assess Sarah's role in all of this?
   - What was the outcome of this second venture: Who was hurt and how?

2. Relationships:
   - Describe the attitudes displayed by each of the three main characters in the first story: Sarah, Abraham, Hagar.
   - Describe the attitudes displayed by each of the three main characters in the second story: Sarah, Abraham, Abimelech.

3. Your central issue: For Abraham and Sarah, the central issue of their lives was their childlessness. So much revolved around this problem. Is there a central, defining issue in your life? If so, what is it and how have you responded to it? Here are some options:

- a need/desire to please
- laziness; a lack of perseverance
- the need always to be right
- addictive behavior
- not being faithful
- fear
- abuse in childhood
- illness
- struggle
- fear of death

- a call to love
- desire to succeed
- a relationship
- desire for God
- loyalty/faithfulness
- trust
- desire to help others
- great energy
- restlessness
- ambition

4. Your relationships:
- What do you most closely identify with in these two stories?
- What characterizes your relational history?
- What are your key attitudes in relationships?

Optional: Discuss the following observation by the famous scholar G. Von Rad: "The bearer of the promise is the greatest enemy of the promise."

Pray (5/10 minutes)

End your time with prayer together in a manner which is appropriate to your group. Pray about:
- finishing the spiritual autobiography: that each person will find the energy to do so; that the process will reveal useful information concerning each person's pilgrimage;
- relationships: that we are clear about the key people in our relational world; that we are clear about the positive and negative parts of our relationships; that we grow in our ability to love and forgive others;
- issues: that we find the central, defining issue in our lives, if such a thing exists for us; that we understand how this issue has shaped us; that we learn how to trust God in the midst of that issue.

Homework

By this stage you are aware of what you do and do not remember about your spiritual journey. Start consulting outside sources in order to fill in the details of your memory: journals or friends and relatives who were with you at crucial points and who know your spiritual history. Continue to pray about this project and be alert to sudden insights or memories. Do not forget why you are writing a spiritual autobiography. It is not to complete an assignment or to do a project for the sake of itself. This is an exercise (a discipline, actually) that helps you learn to notice God's presence.

Testing

Preparing for Sharing: Next week you begin sharing your spiritual autobiographies. This sharing is what this small group series is all about. In this session you will discuss the details of how the sessions will be conducted.

Bible Study Theme: God now asks Abraham to do the hardest thing he has ever done: to give up his beloved son Isaac. This is the supreme test for Abraham. We may have trials on our pilgrimages as well. Of course, challenges come in many sizes and many forms. What is common in all of them is that as we go through them, God wants us to trust him.

Session Aims: The purpose of this final preparatory session is to:
- get ready to share our spiritual autobiographies;
- do a Bible study on hard moments in pilgrimage (Genesis 22:1–14).

Stories (20 minutes)

Challenges

We thrive on them. We avoid them. We seek them out. They frighten us. They exhilarate us. They test us. We love them. We hate them. Challenges are simply part of life.

1. If you had to pick one of the following challenging sports to try, which one would it be and why? Which sport would scare you the most? Why?
   - ❏ parachuting
   - ❏ hang gliding
   - ❏ mountain biking
   - ❏ ultralight flying
   - ❏ white water rafting
   - ❏ scuba diving
   - ❏ rock climbing
   - ❏ sea kayaking
   - ❏ bungee jumping
   - ❏ solo ocean sailing

2. What is the most frightening thing you have ever done? Describe it to the group. *White Water rafting*

3. What is your response to challenges?
   - ❏ No thank you!
   - ❏ Why?
   - ❏ Find someone else
   - ❏ Who—me?
   - ❏ Let me at it!
   - ❏ When do we start? ✓
   - ❏ Let me prepare ✓
   - ❏ Let's see if I can do it
   - ❏ Maybe. . .
   - ❏ I'll do it with the help of some friends

Discuss (15/20 minutes)

Starting to Share Your Spiritual Autobiographies

This is the final Bible study. Next week the first group member shares his or her spiritual autobiography. Go over the details of what that will be like.

1. Schedule: Make sure everyone is clear as to the schedule: who shares when, and who leads when.

2. Leading a sharing session: make sure everyone understands the process (Open; Presentation; Discussion; Prayer). Review the outline on pages 35–37.
   - Discuss the role of the small group leader (page 35)
   - Discuss the process of sharing a spiritual autobiography
   - Discuss the role of each group member (pages 36–37)
   - Discuss the time schedule

3. The final session: look over the material on pages 38–40. Even though the final session is some time away, start to think about your final celebration together.

Study (20/40 minutes)

This story is the high point in the relationship between God and Abraham. It is all about the tension between testing and provision. It is about the conflict between command and promise. In this story Abraham is found to be faithful to God. And God is shown to be faithful to Abraham. This is a hard story because it occurs in such a different context from our own. We cannot even imagine something like child sacrifice. But Abraham lived in an environment where sacrificing a first-born child to a god was a reality. Furthermore, we now know conclusively that God does not call us to kill. Abraham was beginning to learn this lesson (the Ten Commandments had not yet been given). Read this story with all of its genuine horror, but read it also as the story of a God who is teaching significant lessons to the nations through Abraham.

Genesis 22

Some time later God tested Abraham. He said to him, "Abraham!"

"Here I am," he replied.

Then God said, "Take your son, your only son, Isaac, whom you love, and go to the region of Moriah. Sacrifice him there as a burnt offering on one of the mountains I will tell you about."

Early the next morning Abraham got up and saddled his donkey. He took with him two of his servants and his son Isaac. When he had cut enough wood for the burnt offering, he set out for the place God had told him about. On the third day Abraham looked up and saw the place in the distance. He said to his servants, "Stay here with the donkey while I and the boy go over there. We will worship and then we will come back to you."

Abraham took the wood for the burnt offering and placed it on his son Isaac, and he himself carried the fire and the knife. As the two of them went on together, Isaac spoke up and said to his father Abraham, "Father?"

"Yes, my son?" Abraham replied.

"The fire and wood are here," Isaac said, "but where is the lamb for the burnt offering?"

Abraham answered, "God himself will provide the lamb for the burnt offering, my son." And the two of them went on together.

When they reached the place God had told him about, Abraham built an altar there and arranged the wood on it. He bound his son Isaac and laid him on the altar, on top of the wood. Then he reached out his hand and took the knife to slay his son. But the angel of the LORD called out to him from heaven, "Abraham! Abraham!"

"Here I am," he replied.

"Do not lay a hand on the boy," he said. "Do not do anything to him. Now I know that you fear God, because you have not withheld from me your son, your only son."

Abraham looked up and there in a thicket he saw a ram caught by its horns. He went over and took the ram and sacrificed it as a burnt offering instead of his son. So Abraham called that place "The LORD will provide." And to this day it is said, "On the mountain of the LORD it will be provided."

1. The test:
   - What, exactly, does God ask Abraham to do?
   - How does Abraham feel about Isaac?
   - How does Abraham respond to this command?
   - How do you think Abraham might have resolved the conflict between God's promise (that through Isaac will come a great nation) and God's command (to sacrifice Isaac)?
   - What is the test?

2. The provision:
   - What is the temptation for Abraham?
   - What is the provision by God?
   - What does Abraham learn about himself from this? About God?

3. Your testing:
   - In what ways have you been tested on your pilgrimage?
   - Which is harder for you: testing (relying on God in hard circumstances) or temptation (turning your back on God to do what you want)?

4. Your provision:
   - In what ways has God provided for you?
   - How have you experienced the reality of 1 Corinthians: "God is faithful; he will not let you be tempted beyond what you can bear. But when you are tempted, he will also provide a way out so that you can stand up under it." Be specific if you can.
   - In the midst of testing and provision on your journey, what have you learned about yourself? About God?

Optional: Discuss the following statements by Walter Brueggemann in his commentary on Genesis: "[Testing] occurs only in a faith in which a single God insists upon undivided loyalty, a situation not applicable to most civil religions. Testing is unnecessary in religions of tolerance. The testing times for Israel and for all of us who are heirs of Abraham are those times when it is seductively attractive to find an easier, less demanding alternative to God."

"In a world beset by humanism, scientism, and naturalism, the claim that God alone provides is as scandalous as the claim that he tests."

Pray (5/10 minutes)

End your time with prayer together in a manner which is appropriate to your group. Pray about:

- finishing the spiritual autobiographies: that each person will find the resources to do so; that the outcome will be more than worth the effort; that the process will stimulate spiritual growth.
- presenting the spiritual autobiographies: that the first presenter next week will be given special grace; that his or her spiritual autobiography will set the proper tone for all of the presentations; that you will as a group know how to respond in affirming and insightful ways.
- testing: that we will be strong in the midst of our trials; that we will find God faithful in what we face; that we will be given the resources we need to go through our trials.

Homework

Put the finishing touches on your spiritual autobiography. You might try timing the presentation. Most people have more material than they have time to present it. Edit your presentation until you get down to the root issues. And remember: you are not in competition with anyone. Your story is your story. It does not have to be the most interesting or the best told or the most creative presentation. Simply be yourself. Do your best. No one is grading you; no one is judging you. Use this opportunity to further your spiritual growth.

Presenting a Spiritual Autobiography

Preparing for Sharing: What follows is an outline for a typical session in which one person presents a spiritual autobiography. This is the pattern that you will use each week until everyone has shared his or her spiritual autobiography.

Theme: Writing a spiritual autobiography usually brings great insight. We notice patterns in our lives that we have never seen before. We understand better who we are and where God is leading us. We are clearer about our purpose on this planet. This is good. But it is even better to share our spiritual autobiography with others. Sharing our spiritual story deepens our insight. It is as if in making our private musings public we accept who we are in a new way. Private and public selves merge into a healthy unity. Receiving feedback from friends who have heard our spiritual autobiography is very affirming and insightful.

Session Aims: The purpose of a spiritual autobiography session is to:
- focus on the story of one group member;
- interact with that story;
- pray God's blessing on the person who shares the story.

The Role of the Small Group Leader:

It is important to be clear about the roles of the two central people in a spiritual autobiography session. The focus is, of course, on the one who presents his or her spiritual autobiography. However, there is also a small group leader whose task is to create an encouraging environment for the presentation of the spiritual autobiography. Specifically, the small group leader:
- opens the small group session by leading a brief time of prayer.
- watches the clock so that there will be adequate time for discussion following the presentation of the spiritual autobiography.
- guides the discussion after the presentation of the spiritual autobiography.
- leads the closing prayer time.

Opening (5 minutes)

Spend a few minutes praying together. Pray for:
- God's guidance;
- a comfortable and relaxed presentation;
- clarity on the part of the presenter;
- good discussion, filled with affirmation and insight.

Presentation (30/45 minutes)

This is the heart of the session: the presentation of a spiritual autobiography by one group member.

The role of the presenter is to:
- Share a well-prepared spiritual autobiography;
- Be honest in accordance with the level of trust in the group;
- Be disciplined enough to end in time for discussion;
- Be open to the discussion that follows.

The role of group members is to:
- Give the presenter your full attention (to listen in a focused manner—as opposed to merely hearing someone—is a great gift).
- Be affirming in your body language (how you listen helps—or hinders—the presenter).
- Listen with the following questions in mind:
  a. What strikes you about this story? What is similar to your own experience? What is quite opposite from it? (In other words, listen to that person's story in relationship to your story, note the similarities and differences, both of which provide points for discussion.)
  b. What do you learn from the story? What new insights are there for you?
  c. What are the unique and special features about the presenter? What special gifts do you see in his or her life?
  d. If you made a sanctified guess, into which areas of ministry might God lead the storyteller? What might be his or her place in the work of God's kingdom?
  e. What, if anything, puzzles you in this story? What would you like to understand better?
- Do not interrupt (allow space for silence).
- Do not interpret. It is not your job to explain, correct, suggest, or criticize the life of another person.

Discussion (15/30 minutes)

The most common problem in a spiritual autobiography session is the lack of time to discuss what has been presented. There are various reasons for this:
- Who can compress an entire life into 15 to 30 minutes? The challenge for the presenter is to select the key issues/incidents/insights to share and to set aside others. The hardest thing is to decide what to leave out of your story.

- The fear of judgment: Sometimes the feeling is that if I use up all the time then no one can criticize me for how I have lived. This is an unwarranted fear. For one thing, in the covenant everyone specifically agrees "not to judge others, give advice, or criticize." For another, after hearing a person's story honestly told, our desire is not to criticize but to care.

- Bad time management skills: We simply forget the clock. There is so much to say. This is why the small group leader has the task of watching the clock and reminding the presenter when time is almost up.

- Affirmation: When the presentation is finished, begin the discussion by going around the circle and asking each person to identify, very briefly, one element of the presentation he or she most appreciated. Continue this spirit of affirmation throughout the discussion.

- Resonance: Next, using the listening questions (on page 36), discuss the story itself, including what you heard in the presentation that connects with your story. The point of the interaction is mutual sharing, mutual discovery. We learn from one another. Often others "see" for us. We discover that God is working in our lives by noting God's work in the lives of others.

- Response: Near the end of the discussion, allow the presenter to respond. (He or she may have already been doing this in the course of the interaction.)

Pray (10 minutes)

The purpose of this time of prayer is to ask God's blessing on the person who has shared his or her story. This act of blessing is a great gift we can give one another.

Here is one way in which you can pray:
- *Affirmation:* Go around the circle and allow each person to name one thing he or she has come to appreciate about the presenter.
- *Prayer:* Then spend a few moments in prayer, thanking God for the presenter and asking God to guide them as their life unfolds.
- *Blessing:* Gather around the person and have each member lay hands lightly on the person (or someone who is touching them). Ask God to bless them and empower him or her to be God's person and do His will.

There are other ways in which to pray. These include:
- If you feel uncomfortable laying hands on the person, join hands in a circle and pray for the presenter.
- Combine the time of prayer and the time of blessing for the person.

Celebration

Preparing for Celebrating: What follows are suggestions for conducting a final small group session once everyone has shared his or her spiritual autobiography. This is an important session because it provides a chance to bring closure to your small group and an opportunity to plan future small group activities.

Theme: Sharing spiritual autobiographies draws people together. This kind of sharing can be very intense as we confront ourselves, as we identify issues we have faced and must still face in our lives, and as we discover or reaffirm the calling God has for us. But after the intensity of sharing comes the joy of celebration.

Session Aims: The purpose of this final session is to:
- enjoy one another;
- remember together the experience of preparing and sharing a spiritual autobiography;
- plan for the next small group series;
- say goodbye in the context of prayer and affirmation.

Celebration

There are various ways to celebrate your time together. These could include:
- Food: Make this a party. You could do a potluck supper or serve fancy desserts. Maybe chips and soda fit the style of your group. It does not matter what you eat, but be sure to include food. Eating food together is always a rich experience. Food is central to celebration.
- Reminiscence: This is the time for recalling fond memories of the time you spent together. While telling your stories to one another you have also created new stories.

There are different ways to reminisce. You might want to ask people to share their favorite memories from the group sessions or, perhaps, to talk about the most memorable meeting from their point of view. Or you could laugh together about who played which role during the sessions. You might want to discuss the high point and the low point of your time together. If you want to do a small group exercise, you can give "awards" to each person.

- Awards: Take a few minutes and ask each person to decide which "award" goes to which person. Then focus on one person in the group and let the others give their "awards," explaining the reason for the selection. (You might want to do this in sub-groups of four.)

Possible awards include:
- The funniest spiritual autobiography: _____
- The shortest spiritual autobiography: _____
- The longest spiritual autobiography: _____
- The most literate spiritual autobiography:_____
- The spiritual autobiography that would make the best novel:

  _____
- The spiritual autobiography that would make the best movie:

  _____
- The honesty award: _____
- The graciousness award: _____
- The coolness award: _____
- The best listener award: _____
- The liveliness award: _____
- The (_____) award:_____

What's Next?

Discuss the next step for your small group. Here are a few possibilities to talk through as a group:
- SPIRITUAL DISCIPLINES *series:* Take a short break as a group (two weeks) and then start up again and work on another spiritual discipline. There are four other books in this series (see page 81). The next one is *Contemplative Bible Reading: Experiencing God Through Scripture.* In these sessions you will learn a new way of Bible reading (an ancient monastic practice called *lectio divina*) and see how the great stories in Scripture shed light on your story. The other three topics in the SPIRITUAL DISCIPLINES series are: spiritual journaling, meditative prayer, and spiritual transformation. Call Pilgrimage Publishing at 800-476-8717 to order books.
- *Bible Study:* You might want to continue to meet as a small group but switch to a Bible study. Call Pilgrimage Publishing at 800-476-8717 for suggestions about which materials to use.
- *Retreat:* Go on a retreat together. In most areas there are retreat centers that allow you to do silent or guided retreats. This is a great way to deepen your relationship with God.
- *Multiply:* If this has been a meaningful experience for you, why not start other Spiritual Autobiography groups? Work together in teams of two and recruit new members. You and your partner can continue to work on your spiritual autobiographies so that the next time you present them they will contain even more insights. If you feel the need for more training as small group leaders, call the Pilgrimage Training Group at 800-477-7787 to find out the date and time of a one-day small group leaders seminar in your area.
- *Teach:* Instruct others in the process of spiritual autobiography in a Sunday school class or during a one-day seminar.
- *Conclude:* It may be time to bring this particular small group to a close. If you do, you might want to discuss each member's plans for spiritual growth. You might also want to schedule a reunion dinner for a few months from now. Conclude the group with prayer for each other's spiritual pilgrimages.

Prayer/Farewell

End with a final prayer and commissioning service. There are various ways to do this:

- *Group prayer:* Join hands and spend time in prayer together, committing the whole experience and each person to God. Or. . .

- *Testimony:* Ask each person to express one new thing God has said to him or her as a result of this spiritual autobiography small group experience. Then gather around that person, lay hands on him or her, and pray God's blessing on them. Or. . .

- *Affirmation:* Focus on one person. Allow the other group members to express briefly what they have come to appreciate in that person (e.g., his or her courage, honesty, ability to empathize, commitment to ministry, ability to love, practical good sense, friendliness, wisdom, etc.). Then gather around that person, lay hands on him or her, and pray God's blessing on them. Or. . .

- *Liturgy:* Prepare a final liturgy (as a group or by assigning this task to one or two people) using both the ancient prayers of the Church and new prayers written for the group. Use this as the final experience together.

Chapter One

The Content of a Spiritual Autobiography

What, specifically, does a person write about in a spiritual autobiography? How is a spiritual autobiography organized? What is the process by which a person discerns the key issues that make up a spiritual autobiography? What follows is a three-step outline for writing a spiritual autobiography. Use it to guide your preparation. However, remember that the important thing is not that you have followed someone else's instructions, but that you describe your own particular life in a way that reflects who you are in relationship to God.

Step One: Divide Your Life Into Periods

Each person's life can be divided up into a series of interconnecting periods of time. The advantage of dividing a life into periods is that it is much easier to work with a time frame of a few years than with an entire life of many years. Furthermore, if you do the dividing right, each period will have a theme to it. It will have an inner consistency that ties it together in some way. This theme will enable you to make sense out of that particular period. So the first step in writing a spiritual autobiography is to divide your life into a series of different periods. There are two ways to do this: periods based on age, and periods that reflect your search for God.

Age-Based Periods

The first way of dividing your life is to think of it in terms of the various stages we all go through as we grow up. These different developmental periods have different characteristics. The three time periods I suggest are self-evident:

▶ **Childhood:** This is the period of time from birth to the onset of adolescence. Childhood is that time when a person is dependent upon his or her parents and finds their identity primarily in being a member of a family and not as an individual. Childhood is meant to be a tranquil, carefree time in which we are open to God in many different ways. Unfortunately, childhood is often filled with stress and pain which a person must eventually deal with, often as part of a spiritual pilgrimage.

▶ **Adolescence:** Adolescence is a product of both physical and psychological factors. The goal of an adolescent is to break free from his or her family and establish an independent identity. This task is often accomplished amid great turmoil. Adolescence is often a time of real openness to God. More conversions occur during this period of life than any other.

▶ **Adulthood:** This is the rest of life! Adulthood, too, has its unique developmental stages:

- Young adulthood, when the task is to be educated or trained, find a job, leave home, and start your own life.
- The thirties are typically spent raising a family and developing a career.
- Mid-life brings a sharp change from an external focus (on making a place in the world) to an internal focus (finding purpose and meaning) and is sometimes marked by crisis. The questions raised during this time period are often spiritual in nature.
- The fifties ought to be the time to enjoy the fruit of your labor while you give more time to help others, which is often a reflection of your spiritual commitments.
- Retirement is marked by more freedom but less energy to enjoy that freedom! This is a time of summary; of drawing together the meaning of a life and expressing it in creative ways that reflect the wisdom gained through the pilgrimage.

Sub-Categories

It may be useful for you to divide these three major time periods into subdivisions. For example, suppose that during your childhood you lived in two different places: New York City and Cooperstown, N.Y. During the first part of your childhood your family lived in Manhattan, where your parents worked in advertising. But when you were eight they quit their jobs and bought a country inn outside Cooperstown, where they catered to a steady stream of visitors to the Baseball Hall of Fame. So the first half of your childhood would have been spent in an urban environment and the second half in a rural one. Each period would have its own characteristics and should, therefore, be considered separately.

Sometimes the phases in our lives have more to do with people than with places. Here is another hypothetical example. At first, the central people in your life were your parents. But then your dad died and you went to live with your grandmother. Your grandmother became the most important person in your life until you joined a group of friends in the neighborhood and they became the center of your relational life. In this case, there would be three sub-periods during childhood, revolving around parents, grandmother, and friends.

You can make the same kind of divisions within each developmental period. Locate these sub-divisions by looking for themes within a period. The two examples above concern places (moving from one location or environment to another) and people (centering your relational life around a new person or group of people). In addition to places and relationships you might look for new educational experiences (i.e., going to graduate school or taking a painting class); new groups (i.e., joining the Army or getting involved in Young

Life); and new ideas (i.e., becoming a hippie or an atheist) as ways of understanding different periods of time in your life.

Another way of thinking about subdivisions in your life is to look for what might be called boundary events. A boundary event is something new that launches you into a new phase of life. Before that event you were living in one period; after the event your life moves in a new direction. You may only realize that this has happened after the fact. Examples of boundary events are: marriage, the birth of child, an accident, a new job or a new place to live, college, military service, or some other new experience (a new relationship, starting work on a book or some other creative project).

It is perhaps most important of all to divide your adult life into its various phases. How many divisions you have will depend upon your age. If you are in your fifties when you do your spiritual autobiography, you have more periods to look back on than if you are in your twenties.

Determine the subdivisions that make the most sense out of your life. Divide your life into a series of periods (each with some organizing theme) that are short enough to be explored with ease, but long enough to have rich content. Divide your life into eight to twelve time periods.[1]

Search-Based Periods

There is a second way of dividing your life, one that makes particular sense when writing a spiritual autobiography. You can think of your life as different periods that represent the various phases of your search for God. In this case, you would tell your story by discussing how you looked for God, how you gave yourself to God, and how you now follow God. There are three periods that typically characterize the search for God:
- Quest: when you sought to know God
- Commitment: when you came to know God
- Incorporation: when you live your commitment to God.

This is not to say that each person goes through each of these phases. The three phases are typical, not definitive. Likewise, the search for God goes on in so many different ways that it would be foolhardy to suggest that everyone follows this pattern. Furthermore, the time period for any of these periods varies greatly. For some people, neither Quest nor Commitment describes what they experience. If they grew up in church and always believed in God, their only phase is Incorporation. For others, this three-part model is concentrated on Quest. It took years to find God. They have only recently come to know God. For still others, their central problem was commitment. They knew about God; they were convinced of God's reality, but they ran from God for years. It was only gradually that they were drawn into commitment to God.

The Quest Phase

The foundational question in the Quest phase has to do with the direction in which your life is pointed. Is it pointed toward God or away from Him? The shift from one direction to the other, whether gradual or sudden, is worth noting in your spiritual autobiography.

There are several typical "stopping places" in the quest to know God. Some of these "places" have names, others do not:
- Believing that there is no God (atheist)
- Wondering if God exists or not (agnostic)
- Functioning as if God does not exist and is not involved
- Believing that God exists but that God is an impersonal Force, not a personal Being (deist)
- Believing in God but paying little attention to Him
- Actively seeking God
- Actively fleeing God
- Actively seeking evil

The important thing is not the name you give to the various stops in the Quest to know God. The important thing is describe the nature of your search for God. What started you on this search? Who or what aided you? Who or what slowed your search? What kept you moving? What were the key events in your quest? Key people? Key insights? Key experiences?

The Commitment Phase

America is a very religious nation, second only to India in its religious practices (according to the Gallup organization). It seems that almost everyone in the United States believes in God. However, the polls also indicate that this belief does not go very deep. The typical American who says he or she believes in God does not know much about religion, nor does his or her lifestyle reflect many (if any) significant differences from the lifestyle of a similar person who does not claim to believe in God (apart, perhaps, from attending a church or synagogue). So the issue of commitment is a real one. It often marks the beginning of a new phase of spiritual life.

Commitment is not a single event, nor does it necessarily happen all at once. Commitment comes in various ways and degrees. For example, for many people their conscious religious life begins with commitment to the ideas of Christianity. This involves commitment to a certain view of reality including ideas such as:
- It is not good to lie, cheat, or steal.
- Fidelity in marriage is the ideal.
- Heaven exists.
- Jesus is an inspired religious teacher whose teachings are true.

These are a few of the concepts that characterize Christianity. Different people will have different beliefs. And they will hold these beliefs with differing degrees of conviction. But believing certain things to be true and living out these beliefs are two different things. So for some people, the next step in commitment is to translate their beliefs into action. Thus, for example, they do not simply say lying is wrong; they begin consciously to tell the truth in their business dealings. They have moved in their commitment from belief to action.

Another form of commitment is commitment to the church. It is not so much a matter of joining an organization as it is a commitment to a community of people. For some, commitment to the community precedes commitment to Jesus; for others, the two commitments are reversed. In either case, the nature of commitment has broadened from the individual to the community.

Perhaps the most dramatic form of commitment is conversion whereby a man or woman enters into a conscious relationship of trust and obedience to Jesus. Conversions may be dramatic (like that of Paul or Saint Augustine) or quiet or gradual (like most people's), but they all have in common a new awareness of Jesus and a new attempt to follow him. Commitment to Jesus includes all of the previous commitments: commitment to the ideas of Christianity, to a lifestyle based on Christian teaching, and commitment to the company of God's people. In fact, it generally involves a deepening of each of these previous commitments. Commitment to Jesus generally marks the dividing line between the Commitment Phase and the Incorporation Phase.

The Formation Phase

We never move beyond this phase. We spend out entire lives learning to be consistent disciples of Jesus. No one ever gets it fully right. In fact, people whom we would label, "saints" are often the first to maintain that they are, in fact, mere novices when it comes to knowing and serving God. So, the Incorporation Phase has, of necessity, various aspects to it. Most of us should view this phase of our pilgrimage as a series of sub-categories. These include:
- Wrestling with ideas
- Finding our calling
- Developing spiritual intuitions
- Seeking to live consistently
- Learning to love
- Moving toward community

Step Two: Examine Each Period

Once you have divided your life into periods that make sense for you, review each period and look for material that is related to your spiritual autobiography. I want to suggest that you look for at least three things:
- Encounters with God;
- Crises of Faith;
- Outcomes of Growth.

Encounters with God

A central feature of any spiritual autobiography is an account of instances in which the presence of God was especially vivid and/or challenging.

These encounters come in various forms:

- *Mystical experiences.* These can be overwhelming or gentle, but each has the clear sense that God was present.
- *Conversion experiences.* In a mystical experience we encounter the living God; in a conversion experience we respond to God in repentance and faith in Jesus. Conversion occurs in different ways in different lives. Sometimes it is quick and dramatic; most of the time a conversion unfolds over time. In either case there is a conscious sense of having opened oneself to Jesus in faith.
- *Charismatic experiences,* where the work of the Holy Spirit is present in healing, by empowering, or in the fruits of the Spirit (love, joy, peace, patience, etc).
- *Daily experiences,* where you notice God in the everyday flow of life.

The central question which you must wrestle with is this: how has God made himself known to me in each period of my life? This awareness will be distinct at different times of life. In childhood, for example, God is often assumed. God just *is.* In adolescence, God is often encountered in the midst of the struggles to know oneself, and so he is known through dramatic encounter. As adults, we meet God in various ways: as we experience love from another person; in discovering God's handiwork in the world around us; in the struggle to find meaning. Reflect on all of the ways in which you have encountered God.

Crises of Faith

We grow through crises. We may not like crises (I certainly don't), but a crisis often stimulates growth. Quite apart from anything else, crises force us to rely upon God. We may know it to be true in a general sense that without God we cannot cope, but mostly we muddle along until something throws us off balance and we have no choice but to reach out to God. So a good way to learn about your spiritual pilgrimage is to identify points of crisis and then to look for God's presence at those points.

There are at least five types of crises that you need to consider in writing your spiritual autobiography:

- The Crisis of Doubt
- The Crisis of Circumstances
- The Crisis of Disobedience
- The Crisis of Depression
- The Crisis of Darkness

Crisis of Doubt

When you have faith, you have doubt. It is that simple. If everything were cut and dry, clear and obvious to everybody, then faith would not be required, only information. But religious issues touch on many matters that are filled with mystery. Who would want to follow a way of life that does not deal with mystery? Where there is mystery, there are questions.

In your pilgrimage you may have encountered questions that engaged you in various ways (ranging from deep distress to mild curiosity). Typical questions relate to such matters as:

- the existence of God
- the reliability of Scripture
- the problem of evil
- the historicity of Jesus' resurrection

Doubt must be faced and dealt with or it diminishes us. We need to confront questions that trouble us and we need to seek answers to these questions. Fortunately, few of our questions are new or unique. Many people have asked them over the centuries. This is not to diminish the pain or power of these questions in our lives. It is to say, however, that there *are* answers because there has been a great deal of reflection on hard issues by some of the world's best minds. We need to avail ourselves of this treasury of wisdom.

> What questions troubled you, and how did you deal with them? In what ways did you grow as a result? How was your pilgrimage affected by these questions? In fact, doubt of one sort or another may trouble you at this moment. How will you deal with it?

Crisis of Circumstances
Life does not always go smoothly. We wish it did. We try to make it so. We seek to control events so we can keep hard times at bay. Or we hide and pretend that all is well. But, in fact, issues will arise:

- a parent dies
- a relationship turns sour
 - illness strikes
- we are cheated
- we are laid off
- a tornado blows through our town

The list is endless. The question is: how do we cope? Often it is our faith that helps us to make it through. The hope at the core of the Christian message makes it possible for us to face what life sends us.

But not always. Sometimes circumstances create a crisis of faith. Our prayers seems to be ignored. We are treated unjustly and there is nothing we can do. Our parents get divorced and life is not the same again. We lose hope, and are unable to cope without it.

> Consider some of the hard circumstances in your life. Look at the spiritual results. In what ways did you grow (or regress)? How did you cope? How could you have coped? What did you learn about God?

Crisis of Disobedience
Many times a crisis is of our own making. We veer off in a wrong direction and there is a price to pay. This is not to say that if we always do the right thing (as we understand it), we will automatically receive the good thing (that we want). In fact, sometimes we must suffer for doing what is right. We live in a universe of consequences.

Yet in our sin we can grow to know God in new ways—if we deal with the issue. We experience forgiveness. We grow in our understanding of life. We learn hard lessons that protect us in the future. When and how did you fail? What happened? What were the results? Where was God?

Crisis of Depression
We find the most challenges in our live on the emotional level. There is a variety of negative feelings that create crises. For example, consider

depression. When we are depressed nothing else matters. We drag ourselves through life. We are unmotivated. We are sad. We can feel ourselves in decline. And we seem so powerless. We can't even pray, although we know that we need to pray. God seems to be remote.

There are answers to negative emotions: therapy that uncovers root causes; healing of memories that relieves pain we hardly knew existed; drugs that restore our chemical balance; loving care from others that brings us gently back to life.

> What did you learn about yourself, others, and God in the midst of your emotional turmoil?

Crisis of Darkness

For want of a better term, I use "darkness" to refer to those issues in our lives that have the mark of evil about them. There are various terms for this: spiritual warfare, possession, evil. The fact is that we will, on occasion, encounter individuals or systems that have a disproportionate and negative power. In such encounters we are reminded that Paul tells us that we wrestle not against flesh and blood but against principalities and powers. When we encounter this sort of evil the temptation is to despair, to capitulate, to compromise, or to surrender. The fact is, we cannot fight these battles on our own. We need prayer. We need the faith and support of others. We need the presence of Jesus.

We often grow in our faith from encounters like this. In a curious way, we sometimes learn more about the supernatural aspect of life when we confront these dark elements and forces. This is a negative witness to truth.

We must be very careful, however, when we speak about encounters with darkness. There is a very real danger of attribution—pointing our fingers at others and calling them evil when, in fact, they are simply motivated by their lower natures. Be very wary of offering "the Devil made me do it" explanation for behavior. Still, to ignore this category is to fail to notice important facets of a spiritual pilgrimage.

Outcomes of Growth

In each period, in each event, try to notice where God was. This is not always easy. But suffice it to say that God uses all the events and circumstances of your life to shape you into the kind of person He wants you to be. This is not always easy. We do not always cooperate with God. In fact, you may find that your pattern is to be dragged by God kicking and screaming into new growth. Nor will your story be one of unrelenting growth. You have ups and you have downs—these too are part of your spiritual pilgrimage.

Let me suggest various types of growth. These can be used as a grid to reflect on what you have learned in the periods of your life. These will help, define the results of your story. Under each category I have listed a series of questions that you can use to assess results in each time frame. Some of these questions will not relate to you. Use what is helpful; discard what is irrelevant.

Intellectual Growth

What we think shapes who we are. How we think is a product of background, environment, education, family, culture, and economics. Our aim, however, is to develop a Christian worldview—one derived primarily from Scripture, not culture. Achieving this end is not easy, nor is it ever complete. Our minds grow constantly. Our hope is that our minds will grow in the direction of truth. To this end, we need to be aware of both *what* we think and *how* we think. In addition, we need to know who and what has influenced our worldview. In this way we can say "Yes" and "No" to this worldview. So an important question in your spiritual autobiography will concern the state of your worldview in each period of your life.

> How has your thinking about reality developed over time? What are the key ideas that shape the way you process experiences? What are the foundational facts upon which your intellectual life rests? What truths would you die for? How do you grow your mind? Who are the people who have influenced what and how you think? What are the core truths that your life is built on? In particular, what are the key theological ideas that give shape to your life?

Emotional Growth

What we *feel* shapes us as much as what we *think.* We need to have a sense of our emotional life, in addition to our intellectual life. The ability to access the emotional side of life varies from person to person, from women to men. Generally speaking, women are more in touch with this side of life than men.

> What is the emotional tone of each period in your life? In particular, how did you feel about God? What did you feel about how you were living, where you were going in life, and what you were doing with your life? The emotional side of life expresses itself most clearly in our relationships: How would you characterize your relationships in each period of time? How would you describe your emotional life now?

Behavioral Growth

> Our actions reflect what we think and feel. They are the product of internal motivations. What was your lifestyle like in each period of time? How did the way you were living affect the spiritual side of your life? How was your lifestyle determined (or not) by your Christian commitment? What behavior helped your spiritual growth; what slowed that growth?
>
> There is often a gap between our thoughts and feelings and the way we act in public. The reason for this is that we learn what is expected of us and we comply with those expectations, regardless of what we might think or feel. In this case, the important data will come from our private—not our public—lives. What is the nature of that gap and how are you dealing with it?

Relational Growth

At the heart of our religious life is a series of relationships. Identify the key relationships in each period and how they have influenced your spiritual identity. Some relationships draw us to God; others pull us away from Him. In some relationships we are the ones who give; in others we are the ones who receive. In healthy relationships there is both giving and receiving. In the end, spiritual life is about relationships. What (and how) have you learned about loving God, loving others, and loving yourself properly?

Growth in Service

A key aspect of the Christian life is reaching out to others in love and service. There is a clear call in the Bible to be committed to the needs of others, especially the poor and powerless. While each person is expected to engage in general acts of charity, we are also called to specific acts of service. In your spiritual pilgrimage, how have you served both inside and outside the church?

Step Three: Describe Each Period

Now we come to the actual writing of your spiritual autobiography. In fact, you may have already produced your spiritual autobiography Through the process of making notes in the previous two steps. Simply review your notes; identify the key incidents that tell your story; decide on the order in which to tell them; determine where you are now in your spiritual pilgrimage; and you are done!

On the other hand, you may need to work on identifying, selecting, and organizing the material for your spiritual autobiography. This is the subject of the next chapter. A spiritual autobiography is simply the story of where God was in each period in your life; how you responded (or failed to respond); and what you became out of all this. At the heart of your spiritual autobiography will be your stories: the incidents from your life that describe where you have come from spiritually, where you are now, and where God is leading you. It is an exciting story and you will grow by discovering and telling it.

---

[1]These seemingly arbitrary numbers come from Ira Progoff and his experience with what he calls a Steppingstone Exercise (see *At a Journal Workshop*). Eight to twelve time periods work best in assessing a life. Too many periods cause us to lose sight of the meaning of the whole, while too few result in periods which are too long to properly assess.

The Process of Writing
a Spiritual Autobiography

The previous chapter dealt with what to say in your spiritual autobiography. What follows are some comments on how to say it.

Making Notes

As you ponder the question which underlies a spiritual autobiography—"Where are the footprints of God in my life?"—you will invariably be struck with certain thoughts, impressions, or insights. Write these down before they are lost. Not only will you preserve these impressions, you will discover new insights but often in the act of writing.

You might want to discuss these insights or impressions with a friend. Some people gain clarity through conversation. Or you might want to read. The ideas and experiences of others can clarify your situation. For example, you remember an especially poignant time in your life. You are sitting in church listening as *The Ode to Joy* is being played. You find yourself transported into a kind of ecstasy. Tears come. Then, as quickly as it came, this "feeling" (though it was more than mere feeling) is gone and you are left with only the longing to be back in that moment. What is the meaning of this experience? What does it signify? Well, this is the sort of experience that C. S. Lewis calls "The Inconsolable Longing." Look for his books. Read *Surprised by Joy* and the sermon called "The Inconsolable Longing." You will understand better what came upon you and what it means. Do research. The more you know about the spiritual experiences of others the better you will assess and understand your own experience.

The Form of Your Spiritual Autobiography

Different people will create different kinds of manuscripts:
- *A complete, edited manuscript:* You may decide to write down your entire story. This might involve the production of several drafts so that the end product could be published as an article. It takes a certain facility with words and a talent for writing to do this. When you present your story you may decide to read it aloud, or you may use the written version as a guide in telling it.

- *Notes:* This is the other extreme: a series of notes, in sequence, to guide the telling of your story. This is what the gifted storyteller will often do. For example, Garrison Keillor who for years has told "Tales from Lake Wobegon" on his weekly radio program simply makes notes and then when he stands before the microphone he lets the tale tell itself. Using this form for your spiritual autobiography means that you are comfortable with the spoken word.

- *A combination of notes and text:* Many people find it's easier to write a fairly complete manuscript without paying much attention to grammar and spelling, and then use the manuscript to make full notes for telling the story to the group.

I would suggest that you start by trying to write a complete manuscript. If this proves to be too cumbersome or too demanding, shift to a note format. But try your hand at writing. You may be surprised at the results. After all, what are you better qualified to write about than your own story?

Organizing Your Story

Most people tell their stories in chronological order; they skip over less important periods and focus more attention on critical events, people, and experiences.

However, there are other ways to tell your tale:
- *Thematically:* Perhaps you discover that there is a thread or theme that describes who you are and what you have experienced. Examples of themes include: Rescue (being lost and being found, not once but many times); Grace (amazing experiences of God's work and presence in a variety of situations); Travel (in all of the places where you have lived something decisive has happened that shaped your knowledge of God); Relationships (yours is a story of crucial relationships: good, bad, and indifferent); Addiction (entering into addictive behavior, noting, naming, and beginning to deal with it; or a life in which a single temptation has been key). Tell your story by sharing a series of vignettes that illustrate how this theme is woven through your life.

Read the spiritual autobiography in Part III of this book. It has been constructed in thematic fashion. However, it is important to know that generally it is harder to communicate in this fashion than in a straightforward chronological sequence. We are used to thinking in terms of events that follow one after the other. It takes much more work to uncover a central theme and then illustrate it, but do not hesitate to try.

- *Metaphorically:* Rather than a theme, there might be a metaphor that captures your story of interacting with God. The story of the Prodigal Son is one such account. You could use each of the sections in that powerful parable to describe a different phase of your story. Or perhaps the pilgrimage of Abraham describes your experience. One of the concerns in the next book in this series (*Contemplative Bible Reading: Experiencing God Through Scripture*) is finding the story in Scripture which interprets your life best.

- *Through the eyes of another:* It may be easier to write in the third person. Tell your story from your mother's eyes (or from the point of view of your guardian angel).

- *As a fairy tale:* "Once upon a time. . ." is the way the best fairy tales begin. Maybe your life is best told in this fashion.

Editing Your Story

The issue is not cutting out embarrassing or indecent elements from your story. The issue is what to omit, given the time limitations you have. No one's story can be told in its entirety in 30–45 minutes. But what you can share are the key elements that will help people understand who you are and how you have known God.

Once you complete your manuscript or set of notes, go back over it and read it aloud. Time yourself. If you have too much material, make some decisions on how to shorten the story. You can:

- Delete entire sections. This is very difficult but you may find that you have two stories that deal with the same issue; if so, one can be deleted. Or you may have to select stories in order of importance, leaving out the less important ones so that the really good ones are told.

- Shorten stories. Rather than cutting out whole stories, you may be able to reduce the length of several stories so that each can be told. However, be careful not to compress a story so much that you lose the heart of it. The power of a story is often in the details. A summary does not work as well as the full story.

- Combine stories. You may be able to connect two stories into a single story, letting each illustrate the common point (rather than making the point through both stories).

In all of this, remember that sometimes "less is more." The truth of a story is, at times, more apparent when it has been cut to it's "bare essentials."

Creative Ways of Telling Your Story

When it comes to sharing your spiritual autobiography, you can read aloud what you have written. Or you can tell your story using notes you have made. But you do not have to do it this way. You can opt for other ways of telling your tale.

For example, perhaps you are an artist. Why not make a series of line drawings that illustrate key incidents in your spiritual autobiography? Then describe to the group what each drawing represents but often in the act of writing. Or you could raid your family photo albums and create a collage of your life from a spiritual point of view. There are a variety of ways to add a visual dimension to your story, limited only by your imagination and skill.

You might want to add an audio element to your spiritual autobiography. This can be anything from segments of songs which were meaningful at different points in your life (get out your old records) to the creation of "The Ballad of My Life" which you sing to the group.

You could redesign your spiritual autobiography as a parable, an epic poem, or a mystery tale. Do not be limited by the genre of biography. On the other hand, do not be so obscure or fictional that the group is hard put to discover the real you.

The important thing is that what you do be appropriate to who you are. Do not get fancy merely for the sake of being fancy. And do not be intimidated by the creativity of others. Do it your way, remembering that words will always be the central mode of communication.

The Use of Humor

Humor is a great tool in communication. To have a wry view of ourselves is a good thing. But some people are better with humor than others. Know your gifts! And do not use humor to hide. Sometimes a joke deflects attention away from a crucial issue. The challenge is to interject notes of lightness at appropriate points in your tale.

How Long Will it Take?

The actual time all this takes will vary from person to person. Some of it, of course, will depend on your age. The older you are, the more you have to report. Some of it depends on how long you have been conscious of the spiritual side of life. In any case, you should work through the following three steps:

- *Step One:* Determine the major periods of your life. This should take less than 15 minutes.

- *Step Two:* Investigate each period of your life. This can take relatively little time (an hour or two) if you are aware of the major events in your spiritual life. If you have to do research, this will take longer (maybe days). In any case, once you have established the periods, write down as quickly as possible all you can remember from each period that relates to your spiritual pilgrimage. Then review each period more slowly, asking: What encounters were there, what crises, what results? Generally you will find that there are specific incidents that stand out. This is really what you are looking for. The best spiritual autobiographies are those filled with stories, rather than a kind of generalized report in which you summarize what you learned.

- *Step Three:* The work you did in Step Two may have already produced a written outline that you can use to tell your story to the group. All the stories and their meanings are there. Now it is simply a matter of assembling this into some sort of chronological or thematic order. By way of summary, you need to end with a report on where you are now in your spiritual pilgrimage and what you think the future may look like. Again, this could take an hour or two, but it also may take days of work.

I have known people who put together a spiritual autobiography in a matter of hours. I have known people for whom this took weeks of hard work. Do what you need to do, given the time and circumstances you are working with.

And remember, your spiritual autobiography is meant to be told, not read. Therefore, the most important thing is to prepare in such a way that the tale will be told well.

Issues in Preparing a Spiritual Autobiography

On Being Honest

It would be wonderful if our lives were filled with sweetness and light so that we could describe what nice people we are and how coming to God was simply a matter of learning how to meet God. Maybe this is your tale, but I suspect it isn't. In fact, your spiritual autobiography may not be a pretty story.

Many of us are better at running away from God than saying "yes" to Him. All of us are flawed and distorted to one degree or another. That's part of being human. We live on a fallen planet—fallen people living with other fallen people. In fact, our fallen state is what engages us in the search for God. We do not, as humanity once did (so Genesis tell us), know God easily and directly. This is what "original sin" means: that humanity severed its tie with God and went its own way. We are all like the Prodigal Son, living in the far country.[1] So in each of our stories, there will be notes of darkness, of betrayal, of willful evil, of lostness, of sin. The story of our coming home to the Father is often a confused, sad, and bleak tale. To pretend that it is not is just that—to pretend. This is not to say that all stories tell of life among the swine (to continue with the Prodigal Son imagery). In fact, our "lostness" may be found in our "righteousness"—our attempts to be "good little boys and girls" who always do the right thing (like the Prodigal's elder brother). The truth of that kind of tale is often the hardest to discover since so much energy has gone into denial, hiding, and pretending that we are good. It is important to remember that fallenness reveals itself in different ways in different people. But it is here, in our fallenness, that we begin to notice the voice of God, and so our sinfulness needs to be described to some extent.

What about the courage to tell our tale to others? Can we really be candid? Do we want to be candid? Should we be candid? These are not easy questions to answer. One thing is clear: we need to be brutally honest with ourselves. That is hard enough. We also need to be candid with at least one other person. When we "tell another," we gain power over what lies in the darkness. Darkness cannot stand the cleansing power of light as John told us long ago.[2] Light diminishes the grip darkness has over us.

This is why you need to be as honest as possible when you share your spiritual autobiography with the small group. A small group where confidentiality prevails and each person tells his or her tale honestly (no one is exempted from the process) is a potent force for change. When we tell our tale in all its ugliness (and with all its grace) and then find that we are still loved, forgiven, and accepted, we find new life. When we know one another in this way, it brings deep connection and warm generosity. It is difficult to dislike others who have given you the gift of their stories.

But there are appropriate levels of honesty. The basic principle is this: do not share information that will hurt others. Beyond that, you need to consider the level of trust that exists within the group. Ideally, each group will grow in its ability to trust. Openness leads to more openness, so that you can share what, perhaps, you have never shared before.

On Dealing with Past Hurt

In writing a spiritual autobiography, you may uncover issues that cause you pain. When you locate an incident from the past that is still sensitive (i.e., it remains an emotional issue), this is a sign that the situation has not yet been dealt with completely. If this is the case, two things are important. First, do not become preoccupied with the painful incident. Do not give it more attention than it deserves. Remember that your primary task is writing a spiritual autobiography. Do not allow one incident to cloud your sense of the whole. Second, resolve to deal with this issue once your spiritual autobiography is written. Write out the incident in full detail in your journal. Make plans in your journal to get help. This may mean discussing the problem with a friend, writing letters of confession or confrontation, or seeing your pastor or a therapist. In other words, deal with the issue but not in the context of the spiritual autobiography.

On Not Becoming Overwhelmed

The whole idea of producing a spiritual autobiography is so daunting to some people that they are tempted to stop before they start. "I can't do this!" they exclaim. "I can't write. I don't know enough about the spiritual side of life. I have nothing to say. I can't remember much about my past. And even if I could, I'm not a good talker. I could never tell all of this stuff to others."

This is fear. It is very real but it should be rejected. Look at your own objections. Write them down on a piece of paper. (It is important to identify fear specifically rather than leaving it on a vague level which you cannot work with.) Now commit these to God. Ask for God's guidance and God's strength in beginning this project.

One of our fears is that we are being asked to write a book: "My Life from a Spiritual Point of View," or something like that. This is wrong. Our only task is to take about thirty minutes to tell our story to others who are there to hear it.

Another fear is that doing this project will take a lot of time, a lot of wisdom, and a lot of skill. In other words, this is something which only very gifted people (or full-time religious professionals) can do. This is simply not the case. First, everyone has a story to tell. No one is overlooked in the activity of God. Second, everyone can tell his or her story. It does not need to be complex or filled with wise insights. It does not have to cover every detail. Simply talk about how you have related to (or run away from) God. Pick a few important experiences and describe them: your first communion, a profound answer to prayer, discovering that God actually knew and loved you. Tell the group about your contact with church groups of various sorts: being part of a religious fellowship at college, finding a church when you moved into a new community, visiting a retreat center. Describe your rebellion against God and the questions about God that you wrestle with.

Don't make this such a big deal that you freeze up!

On the other hand, do as thorough a job as you can, given the limitations of time and circumstances. Producing a spiritual autobiography means different things to different people at different points in their lives. To some, this is a matter of life and death. They must know where they are now (and have been) in their lives, and they pursue that knowledge relentlessly because this is the only way they can make sense out of their lives. For others, this is a good exercise in getting to know others and letting them know you. The spiritual autobiography is the means by which this happens. For most of us, this is a very useful exercise in developing our spiritual lives and discovering the activity of God in our lives. But remember: do what you can and don't worry about what you can't do. A spiritual autobiography is not something you do only once. You can continue to work on this project after the small group ends.

A Checklist for Writing a Spiritual Autobiography

Here is a brief summary of how to prepare and write your spiritual autobiography:

❒ Determine the date when you will present your spiritual autobiography.

❒ Organize your time so that you will not be rushed at the end.

❒ Read the three chapters in Part II of this book and the sample spiritual autobiography in Part III.

❒ Pray for God's guidance. Continue to pray and listen to God throughout the process.

❒ Divide your life into various periods of time (either by age-based or search-based periods; pages 41–45).

❒ Explore each period (the places, people, experiences of each age period; or the three periods of the search for God: Quest, Commitment, and Formation).

❒ Examine each period of time for the high points (encounters with God: mystical, conversion, charismatic, and daily experiences; page 46).

❒ Examine each period of time for the low points (crises of faith: doubt, disobedience, darkness, depression, circumstances; pages 46–48).

❒ Look for the outcomes of growth (intellectual, emotional, behavioral, relational, growth in service; pages 48–50).

❒ Describe each period in writing—either with notes or by writing a manuscript (pages 51–52).

❒ Time yourself as you practice presenting your story.

❒ Delete as many sections as necessary to get your story down to the allocated time: 30–45 minutes (page 53).

❒ Present your spiritual autobiography to your group.

❒ Continue to explore your spiritual autobiography on your own as a way of deepening your understanding of and growing in your spiritual life.

❒ Work on the discipline of noticing God (pages 59–69).

❒ Tell parts of your story when appropriate to as many people as possible.

❒ Add to your story as time goes on.

---

[1]Read the story of the Prodigal Son in Luke 15:11–32.
[2]1 John 1:5–2:2

The Spiritual Discipline of Noticing

The spiritual skill one learns in writing a spiritual autobiography is that of noticing. We learn to notice God's presence.

This is not a natural sensitivity for most people—though there are some who seem to have been born attuned to the supernatural. Most of us, however, need to develop a sensitivity to the spiritual. We need to become open to the many ways in which the Divine affects us. We need to work at noticing God. This is why I call this the discipline of noticing. It takes effort on our part to master this skill. A spiritual discipline is an activity which we practice so that it will become a habit for us and a normal part of who we are. The practice of spiritual disciplines is sometimes misunderstood to be a mark of piety. In fact, it is a sign of need. If we did it easily and naturally, then we would not have to practice the discipline![1]

The aim of the discipline of noticing is to move the spiritual from the edges of our lives to the center. God has created us to live within both the natural and supernatural realms. But because of the fall, our natural habitat has become the world of sense and time. We barely notice the spiritual. So we have to work at recovering this lost sense of the Divine.

The problem, of course, is not that God is hiding and needs to be coaxed out into the open by our prayers and supplications. He is present in our lives. God is active in the world around us. God is willing to be in relationship with us. The problem is not with God. The problem is with us. We are unaware or barely aware of God's presence. So we have to learn to notice.

A spiritual autobiography is a concrete way of noticing God. In this chapter we will examine seven other ways by which we notice the presence and work of God. In some cases, the presence of God bursts upon us (e.g., a mystical experience). We cannot help but notice God. In other cases, we place ourselves in settings that allow us to notice God (e.g., Bible study and prayer). In all of these ways, we grow attuned to the supernatural (in the midst of the natural) and we develop our spiritual lives.

The Seven Ways

Mystical Experience

Sometimes God bursts in on our lives in such a way that even the most indifferent among us cannot miss His presence. These are easy events to note as we write a spiritual autobiography. However, we need to be aware that mystical events can come in various ways:

- *Encounters with God:* In certain instances, a person is confronted with the presence of the divine in unmistakable ways. There is a sense of Presence. Sometimes there is a light, a voice, or a physical phenomenon. For example, in Paul's experience on the Damascus road, a light greater than the Middle Eastern sun flashed around Paul and his companions. He heard a voice which revealed the essence and meaning of his life. His companions were struck to the ground and rendered speechless. There was a sense of Presence. Someone was there, confronting and calling Paul. Paul discovered that it was Jesus who had met him. In his dialogue with Jesus, Paul received a call that changed the rest of his life. Such experiences are unusual (though remarkably widespread—one research study indicates that more than 30 percent of adult Americans have had a mystical experience).[2]

- *Brushes with God:* Not every experience of the Divine is so overwhelming. More common are what might be called mild mystical experiences. For example, in the course of reading the Bible, a text comes alive in an almost tangible way, and you *know* that God is speaking to you. Or, while on vacation you sit in the garden of an old Spanish monastery, and you sense something about that place that rings of the Divine. You rest in that reality for a long time before you move on to your next destination.

- *Longing for God:* This is what C. S. Lewis calls "the inconsolable longing": for an instance, we are drawn away from this world into another world—a world where we find ourselves deeply at home. We discover that this is where we truly belong. But just as quickly as this comes upon us it vanishes, leaving behind a deep longing for what we encountered. We may return to the music, the words, or the place that triggered the experience, but we find only the longing. Lewis would argue that these are genuine intimations that our true home is with God and that someday, God willing, we will live there.

- *Empowerment by God:* The New Testament tells us that we can expect the Holy Spirit to give spiritual gifts to us, among them: hospitality, wisdom, healing, tongues, teaching, etc. The nature, character, and use of these gifts is the subject of other books. Suffice it to say that sometimes we encounter God through these gifts, as recipients (we are healed when someone lays her hands on us and prays) or as practitioners (in the classroom we sense that we are much better teachers than, in fact, we should be; it is as if God is guiding us). By means of charismatic gifts we know God.

- *Relationship with God:* God is alive to us and present for us. God is no mere concept, but a companion. We pray. We listen. There is dialogue. There is awareness.

These experiences change us. We lose our fear of death. We become more loving people. We find our true calling. We set aside lesser things that were once attractive to us. We develop a thirst for the spiritual. Mystical experiences have a prominent place in our spiritual autobiography. What mystical encounter have you had? What role has that experience had in your pilgrimage?

The Bible

I, for one, would like a world where the mystical was normal; where God touched me constantly and deeply so that my fear disappeared, my questions were answered, and I became a deeply spiritual person. But that, alas, is not the way God operates. Were this the norm, I suspect we would have little need for faith. We would simply "know." As it is, we have a sufficient record of God's interaction with our planet and the people on it. This is what lies at the core of the Bible: the revelation of who God is, how we meet and know Him, what reality is all about, and how to become what we were meant to be. "The entire Bible is a record of God's speaking in human history."[3] To understand and absorb the Bible (much less to live it out in our lives) is a long and demanding process. In fact, it takes a lifetime—and even then we will have hardly begun.

How do we notice God by means of Scripture? In the Bible we find:
- *The story of God:* Here we learn of God's interaction with humanity. Through the many stories in Scripture we are alerted to God's presence in our lives. We learn the meaning of our lives. We know where to look for God. In particular, the story of Jesus gives a face to God. Jesus is what God looks like in time and space, living on our planet as a human being.

- *The wisdom of God:* Here we learn how we are meant to live. We learn to see events through a Christian worldview. We gain insight into what is happening around us and how to respond.

- *The challenge of God:* Here we find our calling from God, both in terms of our particular place in God's scheme of things and of the way we should live daily.

- *The praise of God:* Here we find hymns and prayers that have been used for centuries in expressing devotion to God in worship and thanksgiving.

The Bible is the guidebook which opens up to us the work and character of God. It helps us to see Him. It enables us to distinguish between God and other realities. It trains us in the ways of God. What role has the Bible played in your pilgrimage?

Nature

God is the great Creator. This is his planet and we are the people he has fashioned from the dust of the ground. Thus our whole world bears the imprint of God. Of course, the trick is noticing the handiwork of God. One way we do this is by way of metaphor. A metaphor displays an attribute of something else. With metaphor we move from what we see and know to what we do not see and do not know. For example, sitting in the midst of a vast, green meadow, dotted with spreading maple trees, covered with delicate flowers, alive with bees and birds, we learn about the beauty of God. "If God created this tranquil paradise, how much more beautiful and peaceful must God be. . ."

A few years ago I visited the Victoria Falls in Zimbabwe. It is such an improbable phenomenon. Upriver from the falls the mile-wide Zambizi River flows along at a leisurely pace. It is a quiet, steady, forceful African river—suddenly it is confronted with a great gash in the earth. It is as if someone took an ax and plunged it deep into the ground, cutting the river in two. The river, in protest and with great agitation, plunges over the edge and falls hundreds of feet to the canyon below. As it falls over the edge and dives down to the bottom, the water roars and boils. It sends up great clouds of mist and spray. It becomes a wild, enraged torrent before racing through the canyon below and over the cataracts, having been reduced from a body of water one mile wide to a swift and dangerous river a few hundred yards wide. Standing there at the edge of Victoria Falls one cannot help but feel the power of God; the wild, untamed, irresistible power of God. As you peer through the mist, the falls are revealed then suddenly concealed, only to be revealed again in a different way, much like the way in which God's power and presence is hidden and revealed in our lives; hidden only to come at us and a new way in a new place. I am not particularly sensitive to nature and what it tells us about God, but even I could not miss the sense of God's creative power there at Victoria Falls.

We sometimes decry "nature as our church," feeling (rightly) that we need to meet with others on a regular basis to praise and worship God rather than sit alone on a beautiful lake in the early morning. However, in saying this we may miss what is called "natural revelation." This term refers to the fact that we can learn about God by viewing his creation with enlightened eyes. Again, the issue is learning to see properly. We must learn, for example, to distinguish between original creation and fallen creation. The Earth and the people God created were perfect. But then a distorting element was introduced through human disobedience to God and the world was never the same again. A good creation was marred. We need to see beyond the flaws (hurricanes, mosquitoes, disease) to the original (the grandeur of sea and mountain, flowers, giraffes). In what ways have you learned of God by noticing His creation?

Inner Experience

God speaks with the still, small voice within us—that is the testimony of many men and women down through history. How God speaks is the subject of conjecture (through our minds, the unconscious, in sub-audible ways, etc.); *that* He speaks is a matter of experience.

God uses various means by way of conviction:
- An inner sense of rightness. There is a tone, a sense that sometimes comes to us that carries its own weight of authority.
- A divine compulsion (as opposed to a neurotic compulsion), a sense of the "ought" which convicts us.
- An inner voice. When we pray we often receive new insight, we find a wisdom to confront what we are struggling with, or we gain a sense of mission as we listen. If prayer is, indeed, a conversation and not a monologue, we need to learn to hear God's voice and to distinguish that Voice from all other voices.
- Dreams: the men and women of the Bible knew that God could speak through dreams. They assumed this. For example, if Joseph had not known that God could speak through dreams he would not have understood the nature of Mary's pregnancy, nor would he have known he should flee to Egypt with his wife and child to avoid the wrath of Herod. Most dreams are not from God. Some are and these generally have a sense of rightness about them.[4]

Dallas Willard would argue that the "still small voice" (1 Kings 19:12) or "interior voice" "is the preferred or the highest form of individualized communication for God's purposes."[5] This is not so strange when we remember that Paul says: "We have the mind of Christ" (1 Corinthians 2:16).

The problem with inner experience, however, is that it is internal. There is no external validation to what we sense. The danger is that we may attribute to God what is not from Him. On the one hand, we need to learn to recognize the voice of God by being in relationship with Him. On the other hand, we should accept inner urgings with some care, testing them with Scripture (are they consistent with God's voice there?), with the church (does this fit in with tradition?), and with those to whom we are accountable (what do those who know us best say?).

> What experiences of "hearing God" have you had in the course of your pilgrimage? How has this affected you? Changed you?

Worship/Contemplation

If God speaks to us in Scripture and in prayer, then we should set aside time to engage in these practices that are most conducive to noticing God. The rhythm of each person's conscious pursuit of God differs. For some, this involves a daily time set aside for Bible reading, prayer, reading religious texts, contemplation, and worship. For others, the focus is on public worship on a regular basis. Perhaps a weekly small group Bible study is the center of your conscious pursuit of God. Or it may be periodic visits to a retreat center or a spiritual director. The point is not what we do by way of devotional practices, but that we give ourselves some space in which we say, "Speak, Lord, your servant listens" (1 Samuel 3:10).

There is yet another way in which we hear God's words: through the voice of other people. Perhaps the most common experience of this comes in worship. A sermon is preached, and in some way it resonates with us. We understand in a new way; we are challenged to a new path; we grasp a new truth. It is clear in Scripture that God speaks through people. For example, God appointed Moses as his spokesman (Exodus 4). The prophets knew that they spoke the word of God (e.g., Jeremiah 20:9; Micah 3:8). In a lesser way, it is our experience that there are times when we sense we (or others) are saying something that has come from beyond us. The word of God "can and does come to us through the living personality, mind, and body of other human beings as they, in unison with God, speak to us."[6]

> What role has worship (the community seeking God) and contemplation (the individual seeking God) played in your spiritual pilgrimage?

Relationships

Jesus told us the parable of the sheep and goats. He said:

"Then the King will say to those on his right, 'Come, you who are blessed by my Father; take your inheritance, the kingdom prepared for you since the creation of the world. For I was hungry and you gave me something to eat, I was thirsty and you gave me something to drink, I was a stranger and you invited me in, I needed clothes and you clothed me, I was sick and you looked after me, I was in prison and you came to visit me.'

"Then the righteous will answer him, 'Lord, when did we see you hungry and feed you, or thirsty and give you something to drink? When did we see you a stranger and invite you in, or needing clothes and clothe you? When did we see you sick or in prison and go to visit you?'

"The King will reply, 'I tell you the truth, whatever you did for one of the least of these brothers of mine, you did for me.' " (Matthew 25:34–40)

Apparently, we meet God when we respond to others in need. This is, after all, what the Great Commandment is all about: "You shall love the Lord your God. . . and your neighbor as yourself." To be a Christian is to be a member of this community of love where we meet God in one another. It is not that we are all divine or anything like that (God is God; human beings are made in the image of God). But, rather, the Spirit of God works in and through people. We sense the presence of God's Spirit in loving acts of kindness. It is through others that we learn about who God is, how we are meant to live, and what Christian community is all about. And we are changed by these encounters. God has changed us.

What is the role of other people in your pilgrimage? I suspect that this will be a major area of concern in your spiritual autobiography. People affect our journey in all sorts of ways:

- They start us thinking about faith. Who first raised religious questions for you? How? In what ways did they help you take the next steps in your faith pilgrimage?

- They introduce us to Jesus. How did you come to follow Jesus? Who had the greatest impact upon you in this regard?

- They model faith for us. Who are the wise men and women who guided and shaped your pilgrimage? How?

- They care for us in times of need and celebrate with us in times of joy. Who in your community of faith has they nurtured, supported, loved, and rejoiced with you over the years?

- They open themselves to us for care and support. To whom have you reached out in the course of your pilgrimage? In what ways? With what results? How did you grow?

Your spiritual autobiography could not be written without including the names of many others. The Christian pilgrimage is not a solitary journey. It is a matter of walking alongside the Company of the Committed (to use Elton Trueblood's phrase). Our stories are intertwined with the stories of many others. In them we come to know about God and, in fact, to know God through them.

Fruit of the Spirit

Scripture reveals a very concrete way of identifying the presence of God. In Galatians 5:22–23 Paul states that ". . .the fruit of the Spirit is love, joy, peace, patience, kindness, goodness, faithfulness, gentleness and self-control." So when we encounter any of these qualities, in some way we are in touch with the Spirit of God. As we notice these good fruits, we give thanks to God. Likewise, we should seek to display them in our lives. In this way, we yield ourselves to the work of the Spirit.

Think about the times in your life where you have encountered these qualities. Then reflect on the ways in which God was there.

- Love. The affirmation that John makes in his first epistle is that "God is love" (1 John 4:7–12). It not that God *brings* love (he does), not that God *promotes* love (he does), not that God *desires* for us to be in loving relationships (he does). It is that God, in his essence, *is* Love. Thus where love prevails, in some way God is there. In Greek there are four words which, when translated, mean "love." In the Galatians text the word used is *agape,* which refers to actively reaching out to others simply because they are in need, and without regard to reward or response. This is the kind of love which God inspires in us and others.

- Joy is not the same as happiness. Rather, it refers to a deep inner attitude of delight. This joy is not disturbed by hardship. It is connected with hope which knows there is an inheritance waiting for us in God's future.

- Peace is not contentment as much as it is a deep contentedness. The root meaning of this word is not negative ("an absence of conflict"), but positive ("the presence of that which brings wholeness and well-being"). The presence that brings this peace is God.

- Patience is the ability to persevere with people who aggravate or persecute you. It is the ability to bear up under stress. This is not a natural trait!

- Kindness is an attitude toward people, a way of relating to others.

- Goodness is closely related to kindness. It is, perhaps, a more active way to relate to others in word and deed.

- Faithfulness is the character trait of reliability. A faithful person is someone you can depend on.

- Gentleness is another character trait: it is a kind of meekness though not in the spineless way that word is often understood. It is the ability to defuse conflict or find creative ways through conflict.

- Self-control is the ability to master the desire and compulsion for self-gratification.

Each of the first four virtues (love, joy, peace, and, by implication, hope) find their root in God. To display these qualities is to be touched by God. So when we encounter these virtues in other people, we encounter God's Spirit at work. The next three virtues (patience, kindness, goodness) are expressed in relationship to other people. They are signs of love in action. Again, as such, they give evidence of the work of the Spirit. The third set of virtues (faithfulness, gentleness, and self-control) are more personal in nature. They describe Christian character as it ought to be and again mark the work of the Spirit. In your pilgrimage, who are the people who display these traits? How do you learn of God from them?

Each of these seven ways helps us to identify and track the presence of God in our lives. The story of that Presence is the essence of a spiritual autobiography.

Issues in Noticing God

On Being Loved by God

Central to our experience of God is knowing that we are loved by God. The mystical writers have much to say about this (Bernard of Clairvaux, Evelyn Underhill, Julian of Norwich, Ignatius of Loyola). This knowledge, perhaps more than any other, gives focus to our lives. It is one thing to know theoretically that God loves us (because the Bible tells us so) and another to experience that love (in direct and concrete ways). All the above experiences—mystical encounter, worship, fruit of the Spirit, etc.—communicate that God loves us, and communication is at the heart of a loving relationship. To open oneself to God's flame of love is the foundation upon which awareness of God rests.

On the Dark Night of the Soul

A word also needs to be added about what mystical writers have called "the dark night of the soul." This is the experience of God's absence. These writers explain that this experience seems to come to people who are about to move from a kind of spiritual kindergarten to a deeper spirituality. They also say that this experience weans us away from wanting God's presence mainly for the spiritual thrill and security that it (rightly) gives us, to a state in which we simply want God. It is important to notice that the absence of God is felt only because it comes after experience God's vivid presence. We cannot know what we are missing if we never had it in the first place. For most of us, however, the issue is that we *do not know* the presence of God, not that we have *lost* the sense of God's presence.

On Lethargy

If it is true that God is constantly present, that He loves each of us in an individual way (and not just as a generalized group), and that He desires a conversational relationship with us, why do we not spend more time with Him? Why is the development of a "devotional life" so hard for so many of us?

There is no single answer to this question. The issue may be a combination of several factors:

- *No sense of God's presence:* We do not spend time with God because it all feels so impersonal. To read the Bible and to pray seems like a duty, not a joy. It is a kind of pious good works which we are told is beneficial to us. The lack of a sense of presence may be a matter of never having sought a relationship with God. Or it may be a matter of not expecting God to be present, or not knowing what the term "presence" really means.

- *No sense of relationship:* We will relate to God, in some sense, the way we relate to other people. The ability to enter into comfortable relationships varies from person to person and is the product of factors such as early socialization, family dynamics, an introverted versus an extroverted personality type, opportunities for friendships, past rejection, and so on. If you can spend a whole day with your spouse and be content with routine and occasional conversation, little emotion, and no real interaction, then these dynamics will probably be at work as you relate to God.

- *No conversation:* Our devotional life becomes a burden when we do all the thinking and all the talking. Bible study is reduced to learning; prayer to making requests. There is no conversation; that is, there is no silence where we listen for God and are open to Him. But when one's meditations include both speaking and hearing, there is a different quality to them.

- *No time:* Time is doled out equally to all people. The issue is how we use it. This, in turn, is a matter of circumstance and need. Some have little free time because they must work long and hard to survive. Others have little time because they work hard in order to feel good about themselves. Still others fritter away time or give it to lesser pursuits. Seeking God takes time. This does not mean that we have to enter a monastery or convent to find the time, nor that we have to give up high-demand jobs to be spiritual. It does mean that we have to work at finding time. We can find chunks of time if we look: time commuting to and from work; time when we are engaged in routine chores that leave our minds free for other activities; rising a half-hour earlier or going to bed a half-hour later (if we are, in fact, getting adequate sleep); shifting from an exercise bike to a long walk; the final twenty minutes of lunch break; etc. We can also find time through the choices we make. We can watch television each night but we may choose one evening away from the tube. We can read on a regular basis but we might choose less leisure reading. I suspect that in the rush of contemporary life we will have to discover new ways of seizing time for our relationship with God. In fact, we may not find the time to sit and be with God. Rather, we may learn to speak with God while we are engaged in routine tasks.

- *No routine:* Those who are strong "J's," to use a Myers-Briggs term (J's are people who need order, control, and routine) will struggle with knowing God unless they include him in their routine. Strong "P's" (the more spontaneous types, such as Saint Francis was reputed to be) can seize the moment; "J's" have to schedule the moment.

A Way to Begin Noticing

How do we begin the practice of noticing God? One way is by using the prayer of examen. This is a way of prayer developed by Saint Ignatius, originally for use by the Jesuits (the mission order which he founded). Noticing God is one of the aims of this prayer. It helps develop in us a greater awareness and sensitivity to the concrete ways in which God has been working in our lives over the past day. The more acute our sense of God's work, the better we are able to respond to Him. Using the prayer of examen is a concrete way to begin practicing the discipline of noticing.

The prayer of examen is a three-part prayer process.[7] It begins with gratitude. We scan the previous twenty-four hours in order to notice the gifts which God has given to us. We thank God for all of this. Then, second, we review the previous day and seek to notice the presence of God. We ask the Holy Spirit to show us in the everyday events of the past day where and how God has been present and working in us. Then finally, on the basis of our gratitude for the gifts of God and our awareness of His work, we go back and examine our day a third time. This time we ask the Spirit to show us the ways in which we have failed to respond to God or not lived up to our calling as Christians. We ask to know our sin and failure. Because we come to sin and failure through the path of gratitude and awareness of God's presence, we are able to face and own these shortcomings; we know that even in the midst of them God still loves us and is at work in our lives. We do not make light of our shortcomings. On the contrary, the more we are aware of God's active love for us, the more sorrow we feel for our refusal to respond; the more effort we make to follow God. But we do this out of gratitude, not guilt.

The discipline of noticing is not an isolated activity, unconnected with the rest of our spiritual life. It is part and parcel of that life. As we practice other spiritual disciplines (such as the disciplines of prayer, worship, study, meditation, service, and celebration, not to mention the discipline of spiritual autobiography), we learn the discipline of noticing. This is as it should be. In all, this we need to remember: a spiritual discipline is never an end in itself. It is a means to an end. That end is loving God and enjoying him forever.

---

[1]See *The Spirit of the Disciplines* by Dallas Willard for a discussion of the nature of spiritual discipline.

[2]There are numerous examples in the Bible of this sort of phenomenon: the fire from God which passed through Abraham's sacrifice (which we studied in the third Bible study); the call of Moses in the burning bush (Exodus 3:3–6); the call of Isaiah (Isaiah 6), etc. In addition, there are many examples of individuals who are addressed by angels. For example, Abraham in Genesis 18–19 (see also Hebrews 13:2, which says we may entertain angels unaware); Joshua (Joshua 5:13–15); Daniel (Daniel 9:20–27), Mary (Luke 1:26–38), and Peter (Acts 5:19–20).

[3]*Listening to the God who Speaks* by Klaus Bockmuehl (Colorado Springs, CO: Helmers & Howard, Inc., 1990), p. 13.

[4]There are many examples in the Bible of God speaking through dreams and visions: Abimelech (Genesis 20), Jacob (Genesis 28), Joseph (Genesis 37), Nebuchadnezzar (Daniel 4), Paul (Acts 16:9), Peter (Acts 10:9–19)

[5]*In Search of Guidance* (San Francisco: HarperCollins, 1993), p. 91.

[6]Ibid. Willard, p. 101.

[7]Though it is sometimes described as having five aspects or moments (gratitude, light, the account, deepening, and forearming), I have focused on what seem to be the three key movements.

PART III—SPIRITUAL AUTOBIOGRAPHY

Outlining a Spiritual Autobiography

In order to make this a bit more concrete, I have included an outline of my spiritual autobiography. These are the kinds of notes I could make use of if I were to present my story to a small group. Since I have lived 50-plus years, I would have to be selective about what to include, depending upon how much time I had for the presentation.

The first step in this process was to define the various periods in my life, which I did using age as the main criterion (but adding information about location, work, and ministry). Next, I identified key incidents of various sorts (encounters, crises, growth) in each period. The brief notes give the gist and meaning of the incidents. They are adequate to trigger memories and stories which I can share with a group.

1. Childhood/Detroit
- Age 5: Mystical encounter with God. I remember sitting on my bed. It was afternoon. I was overcome by a sense of the presence of God. I remember saying to God that I would "speak for him." I did not know what this meant. I was frightened and overwhelmed.
- Age 11: Going forward. Following a Bible verse memory contest (in which I won a new baseball glove), our teacher told us how to receive Jesus. He asked us to pray a prayer silently to ourselves if we wanted to receive Jesus. But then he asked all the boys who prayed this prayer to go with him into another room. I wasn't sure I liked that—admitting to everyone that I had asked Jesus into my heart. But I went along and there he explained to us what we had done.

2. Teenage/Denby High School and Ebenezer Baptist Church
- Age 16: Final step in conversion. After my experience at Sunday school I attended the Sunday School only sporadically. My family was away a lot of weekends. In high school I got involved in Youth for Christ. I started attending church with kids from the club. I was elected a youth group officer. But I was still not sure I was really a Christian. This was a time of great doubt and anxiety. Then one afternoon, sitting in the rocking chair in the living room, I claimed the promises in Romans as my own and felt a sense of assurance that I was right with God; a sense that has remained with me.
- Ministry: trying my hand at all sorts of ministry (leadership of youth group, Detroit area Youth For Christ fellowship director, mall evangelism, rescue missions, etc.)—a period of zeal unleashed.

3. Twenties/College & Seminary/Yale and Fuller
- Freshman Year: Returning to my dorm one Sunday evening after church I had the strong sense that I should open the Bible. I did so and my eyes fell on Matthew 28:11–20. As I read the words they came alive. They

were no longer printed words but spoken words, spoken to me. I knew I was to go into missions.

- First Year/Seminary: I met Michael Cassidy. As he talked about his vision for reaching Africa I came to realize that it was my vision, too. During my 3½ years at seminary we organized and launched African Enterprise. Our goal was to preach the gospel in the cities of Africa. I had several experiences of God's presence: in finding a sense of vocation through Ephesians 4:11–13; in finding assurance of calling via John 15:16. It is interesting to me to find how central Scripture had been in hearing God in these early days of ministry.

4. Twenties & Thirties/Africa
- Launching a new ministry: discovering the joys and trials of Christian work; crises of encountering those beyond my circle of Christianity; wondering where God is at times of crisis; learning to work with different personalities.
- Experimenting with ways of outreach; developing small group ministry, media ministry.
- Puzzling over how conversation happens (different people have different experiences); beginning doctoral work by way of investigation.

5. Thirties/Newton, Massachusetts
- The weekly Bible study; learning about small group process and materials;
- Media Production Work: The issue is finding my calling. Is it in media work or direct ministry? The crisis of calling.
- Ph.D.: the continuing investigation; explorations of how we meet God.
- Writing: the nature and logic of pilgrimage.

6. Forties & Fifties/Gordon-Conwell Theological Seminary
- Finding my calling in teaching: exploring ways of teaching; finding all the strands of my background coming together.
- Wrestling with my dysfunctional background.
- Writing Serendipity small group materials: the combination of research, openness to the Spirit; and the voice of the community gathered to study God's Word.
- Exploration of early Christian spiritual traditions; beginning spiritual direction.

7. Fifties/Fuller Theological Seminary
- Renewal of vision; launching new ministries and programs; embraced by an exciting, inclusive community.
- Continuing to explore spiritual traditions.
- Finding God in the world within, in the world without, and in the gathered community.

A Spiritual Autobiography

What follows is an example of a spiritual autobiography. It is not meant to be seen as typical or normative, only illustrative of what a spiritual autobiography can look like. In fact, it is not typical in that:

- It is organized by themes, not in chronological order (though each theme is dealt with chronologically). This spiritual autobiography uses the themes of the Great Command (mind, soul, heart, strength) as the organizing grid. Incidentally, the author's original spiritual autobiography was written in note form, chronologically, and shared with a small group. This version is the product of several years of additional reflection.

- It is drawn from a series of fifteen journals kept by the author. Most spiritual autobiographies draw mainly upon memory with some assistance from conversation and journals.

- It is written. Most presentations to a small group will be based on notes, not on a manuscript.

This spiritual autobiography is included because it demonstrates the depth, the power, the literacy, and the insight that can flow from a thoughtful, carefully crafted piece of work. My hope is that it will inspire you to work with diligence and wisdom on your spiritual autobiography.

By Jennifer Howe Peace

My first journal entry is dated June 11, 1980. I was 13 years old. The opening line reads, "We began our trip at 8:55 Wednesday morning." It was a hot summer when my family (all six of us) piled into the family station wagon and headed cross-country from Boston, Massachusetts, to the California coast. Now, 15 years and 15 journals later, I have once again traveled from Boston to California. As I stand on the brink of a new phase in my pilgrimage—entrance into a Ph.D. program at the Graduate Theological Union—it seems like an appropriate moment to look back at what has led me to this place.

To call my life a pilgrimage I have to answer the basic question: Where am I going? My sense of where I am going has largely been defined by my Christian upbringing. The task for every Christian can be summed up by Jesus' words to the Pharisees when asked which commandment in the law is the greatest. He replied, "You shall love the Lord your God with all your heart, and with all your soul, and with all your mind, and with all your strength. The second is this, 'You shall love your neighbor as yourself'" (Mark 12:30–31).

My journals do not tell the story of a simple pilgrimage from point A to point B. What emerges very clearly in my journals is that there have been several different "pilgrimage sites" which are all part of the larger journey. In the Great Command, Christ names the parts of the self with which we are to love God. These correspond to the "sites" in my own pilgrimage; mind, soul, heart, and strength (or body). The main work (or the path) in each area usually begins when I move to a new place. Each of these pilgrimage sites is associated with a specific geographic location. It seems, as I noted in one journal entry, "New environments allow me to explore parts of myself that I may have previously ignored" (4/30/90). Tracing my journey to each of these "sites" was very illuminating for me in terms of understanding my own patterns of growth.

Mind Pilgrimage (College)

"What an exciting day of intellectual stimulation!" (9/30/86). My journal entries in college are dotted with such exclamations. In college I discovered the power of the mind and I "fell in love" with knowledge. My journal became a repository for my "to do" lists, quotes from various readings, and conversations with my professors about classes and my future goals. I took extra courses and my best days seemed to be when I was busy from morning until night with classes, reading, and writing. It was an exciting period but the intellectual tended to shut out everything else around me.

At the School of Oriental and African Studies (SOAS) in London where I spent my junior year of college, the motto was "knowledge is power." I experienced a growing ambivalence in my relationship to knowledge and I started to question my own motives for pursuing knowledge.

> Is it naive to believe that there is such a thing as knowledge for the sake of knowledge? Our educational structure is founded on faith in the value of knowledge in and of itself. Equally important for any scholar, I think is the understanding that knowledge is power. Knowledge is not a passive agent. Knowledge as power can be used for good or evil. The greatest danger lies in not owning this power (1/30/91).

At seminary I saw knowledge of God and Truth being used by some people to separate and intimidate, and to assume power. In seminary I wrote, "I start feeling very uncomfortable when I sense that knowledge and power are what we worship above love. Knowledge tends to divide those who know from those who don't. Power tends to separate those above from those below. But love connects us, restores us, and gives us hope. Is this not what God offers above all else? Love?" (2/13/91). I understand more about God, myself, and others when I study and probe with my mind, but I am keenly aware that intellect isolated from spirit, heart, and body becomes lifeless.

Soul Pilgrimage (London)

I was brought up to believe in the God witnessed to in the Old and New Testaments. I was a member of the Congregational church in my home town and enjoyed youth group and church service. Once I moved away to college, I realized that faith wasn't something you inherited from your parents and that my personal faith was pretty shallow. I wrote, "I think that my belief in Christianity stems from the fact that I have observed its effects on my parents' lives which I respect."[1] When pressed by a woman in my aerobics class who asked, "Are you a Christian?" I answered, "Well, my parents are. My dad is ordained but, no, I'm not a Christian."

My soul's experience with a higher reality leapt to a new level of consciousness during my year in London. I had a sense that I was embarking on a journey:

> I'm starting something tonight. In response to my letter asking Dad about the Holy Spirit and Christianity, he sent me a book called **Basic Christianity** by John Stott. In it, Stott says that whoever seeks honestly after the Truth, will find it. He challenges me to read a chapter a night from St. John's Gospel and to repeat the following prayer: "Oh God, if you exist (and I'm not sure if you do) and if you can hear this prayer (and I do not know if you can) I want you to know that I am an honest seeker of the truth. My mind is open. I am willing to believe. My will is surrendered. I am ready to obey. Teach me the truth. Show me if Jesus is your son and the savior of the world. And if you bring conviction to my mind, I promise to accept him as my savior and follow him as my lord. Amen." I like that prayer and I am going to take the challenge.

Three days after this entry, I went on a weekend retreat with my godbrother Andrew and some young adults from his church, Holy Trinity, Brompton, a very low Anglican, evangelical church. While there I had a profound, life-changing experience which I traced in my journal:

> I went into the evening service with a bad attitude. Something was said about being drawn together. I didn't feel that anyone had made a particular effort to draw me into the group. The first thing on my note pad was, "We are not drawn together!" Then I took a few notes on the lecture (our identity with our Christian friends). Further down I wrote, "I don't get it, who are these people—coming in and out, leaving for parties? They aren't here to talk to and help others. They are here to pat each other on the back and reinforce what they already know. . .O.K." I decided to try and listen to the lecture but I just wrote down whatever random word I heard for the sake of writing and looking involved, or maybe so I didn't have to look at the obnoxiously sincere expressions on people's faces. But I was soon diverted. Someone read a definition of love from the Bible and said, "If this portrait leaves you breathless, it should." The note on my pad was, "No, the portrait does not leave me breathless." One of the few bits that struck me was when in the closing prayer, Andy said, "I long for you to open me up to your limitless supply of love." I jotted down a little more but then concluded my notes with a big, "STUPID!!"

Then we started singing songs. I was continuously flipping through the list of songs, usually finding the one we were on when we were halfway through it. Of course everyone else knew them by heart. They were basically all the same tune with different words. Suddenly out of the corner of my eye, I saw strange goings on. People were standing, arms out, or by their side, in a trance-like state or weeping quietly. Carla flopped down on the couch, eyes still shut. Others went and stood over her. "What are these people doing?" I asked myself again. I was still fumbling along with the songs and trying to stay as detached as possible from the people and events around me. "Wow," I thought, "these people are emotional wrecks, what are they all crying about?"

Now before this, while I was angrily singing along, I felt moments of welling emotions as though I were about to cry. But I quickly dismissed these feelings because, I firmly told myself, I have nothing to cry about. As I went along, it was more and more difficult to suppress this urge. Then Andrew came over and asked me how I was doing and told me not to be too overwhelmed or frightened by what was going on. That did it, my concentrated resistance was broken and I started to cry and cry and cry. I didn't care any more that I couldn't think of any reason to cry. I just wept with wild abandon (1/9/88).

Thus began a long dialogue with myself and with God as to the meaning of this experience for my life. During my year in London I was intensely focused on the spiritual through prayer, reading, the two churches I attended, and two weekly Bible studies. I later described this period as my honeymoon with religion. Near the end of my year in London, the same woman in my aerobics class who had questioned me when I arrived, asked, "Are you a Christian?" I answered without hesitation, "Yes, I am."

Since this confession of faith in Christ I spent two years in seminary getting my masters of theological studies degree with a focus on comparative religious studies. While there, I revisited my conversion experience and attempted to describe it through poetic prose:

The waves which washed over me brought an intense sense of pain. The tip of the wave brought personal pain and a vision of my weaknesses and faults and fears. But the bulk of the wave brought a greater, more ominous sense of pain. Of the pain of the universe crying out, why? Why do I exist? How can I bear all that's being done? I rocked and roared with the pain of the world. The second wave was equally strong but it brought joy. The tip of the wave reminded me of my life and the lightness I can bring to others. The bulk of the wave brought a warm tender flood of the joy one feels when one is loved. A deep down sense that at the core of all my pain, I am loved, deeply and fully. Even to recall is to reel in wonder. To outside observers perhaps it seemed that I was still simply crying as before. But inside, my body leapt for joy and longed to stay in the arms that held me. The third wave washed me up on shore and left me sobbing slightly from exhaustion. The ocean receded and was lost from my direct sight. But once you know something exists, no fortress can deceive you. I stayed silent, slightly shocked. What had happened? My mind leapt back into control and demanded to know what had

*been going on and who was responsible. Be still mind, I cautioned, this is
beyond the both of us. This will take time. I felt new and young. I felt ancient
and worn. I felt exuberant and exhausted (4/28/91).*

Heart Pilgrimage (Connecticut)

In high school I was extremely social. I had a large group of creative friends
who kept me happy. In college I began to crave intimacy, someone to know
and be known by. My pilgrimage of the heart began with my realization of
how lonely I was in college: "I never let myself think about how lonely I am.
I go through my day totally on my own, bouncing off other people here and
there. I have a lot of associates. Is this what being independent means?"
(10/30/86)[2] Since my first two years in college were years of the mind, I
generally ignored my heart and buried myself in my work.

I soon made some friends at the university and became very involved in
my church. The focus of my year shifted to my soul's pilgrimage and I put
issues of intimacy off. It was after I returned to Connecticut for my senior
year of college, when I least expected it, that I fell in love. Joel lived on my
hall. We developed our friendship through the year and didn't start dating
until a few months before graduation. By then, I had already made plans
to go and live in California for the year, and so Joel offered to drive me. For
me, love was a slow realization rather than a flash of lightning.

Joel and I dated after college and in July 1995 we were married. He has
been the main catalyst for my heart pilgrimage. My relationship with Joel
has forced me to grow in every other area of my life. It has also allowed
me to see more clearly the nature of my relationships to other friends and
members of my family. Most significantly, my love for Joel has opened me
to a whole new understanding of what it means to say that God is love.

Strength Pilgrimage (California)

The struggle to see my body in a balanced, positive light has been a long
and difficult journey. As early as junior high I remember thinking of myself
as fat and ugly. What is most notable in my journals from high school is my
obsession with food. Entry after entry I list the food we had for dinner or
what everyone ordered when we went out for a meal. In college I tried
and failed in several attempts to diet and exercise regularly. I wrote, "I'm
starting to see myself as fat. I wish I had more will power" (9/8/86).

The main work on improving my body image came during my year in San
Jose. I joined Weight Watchers and learned about what my body needed
rather than what it wanted. I joined a health club and began exercising regularly. I started taking a pottery class, something physical, creative, and stress-
relieving. I learned what it felt like to experience my body as light, respon-
sive, and beautiful rather than heavy, slow, and ugly. It was a liberating year.

The "conclusion" of this journey came the following year in seminary
when I used my new body confidence to put together a slide show about

women and body image. The show, entitled, "Women in the Mirror: Reflections of Modern America," was sparked by reading a passage in 1 Corinthians: "Do you not know that your body is a temple of the Holy Spirit within you, which you have from God, and that you are not your own? For you were bought with a price; therefore glorify God in your body" (1 Corinthians 5:19–20). Helping others to see what a burden a negative body-image was, helped me to move further along in my own journey.

Conclusions:

The process of simply reading through my fifteen journals was a pilgrimage in itself. I had a strange sense of time reading in the present tense about my past self. When I read old entries, I re-entered feelings and states of mind. It was very interesting to take a bird's eye view of the past fifteen years of my life. I was overwhelmed by the amount of data and feel that I have just begun to scratch the surface of interpreting it. I realized in writing this paper that each section could have been a paper in itself. But this overview helped me recognize that my pattern of growth seems cyclical rather than linear. The same themes and issues appear repeatedly until the message sinks in. Then just when I think I'm done with a certain area of development, I return to it on another level.

It was particularly interesting to me to identify my mini-pilgrimages and to link them with physical moves. I went to Connecticut College in New London, Connecticut, where I discovered the power of the mind and the seduction of knowledge. My junior year I traveled to the School of Oriental and African Studies and while in London I focused on my soul's pilgrimage. I returned to Connecticut for my senior year and fell in love, beginning the pilgrimage of heart. After graduation I spent a year in San Jose, California, living with my aunt and uncle. The focus and work of this year was on my body/body image. I would say that the years following my time in California have been focused on integrating the work that went on in various aspects of my life and returning to the same themes but on different levels.

Learning to trust my mind, body, and heart has taught me something about the language of the Spirit. God calls us to love with our whole being and the Spirit works through every part of us. I feel God constantly at work trying to move me toward wholeness and harmony. My hope is that I can balance and serve the demands of my heart, soul, mind, and body so that I might continue to learn what it means to love God and to love my neighbor as myself.

---

[1]Journal entry: 12/20/87.

[2]Ironically, this entry was written on my fiancé's birthday, before we had met.

An Introduction to the
SPIRITUAL DISCIPLINES Series

Four themes weave their way through the five books in the SPIRITUAL DISCIPLINES series: story, pilgrimage, community, and discipline. They are interconnected. Each points us toward God. Each gives us a way to relate to the spiritual in life.

Story

We all have a story. Our stories give us identity. They tell who we are since they chart the unfolding of our lives and all of the factors that make each of us unique.

But we do not always know our stories. There are various reasons why our stories remain indistinct or uncomprehended:
- *Inattention:* We let life pass us by. Each day comes and goes, and we hardly notice. Perhaps our routines blind us to what is happening around us; perhaps it is because we live our real lives in another world: a world of books or computers or television. Since our minds are not focused on what is happening in and to us, our days go unchronicled.
- *Pain:* Our lives are too painful to recollect. Not noticing is our way of coping. If we remembered we would cry out in agony. We often get through rough times but then we lock those events away in a dark box, never to see the light of day. If we remember what happened to us we come unglued.
- *No grid:* We do not notice the texture of our lives because we do not have categories for talking about them. Life just happens. We assume that life for us is like life for everybody else. It is not, of course. We need to think about who we are in some organized way. We need to describe and tell our stories in ways that connect with others.
- *No friends:* We do not know our stories because we have never talked about them with anyone else. Perhaps we are shy; or it may be because we do not have friends who we can talk to about such things. Or we may tell only certain kinds of personal stories (e.g., about the kids or job) but keep most of our life private.
- *Cultural shyness:* We do not tell our stories because we have been taught not to do so. Our shyness or reticence is a cultural thing; it is the way we were raised.

If we do not know our stories, we cannot understand them. If we do not understand our stories, our lives remain a mystery to us. We do not understand our anger, our needs, or even our desires. We cannot anticipate our responses or plan our futures. We are left with only the immediate here and now, and that, too, soon passes off the screen of our consciousness.

In addition we have no way of making sense out of our stories. We do not think they have any significance beyond ourselves. We do not connect our stories with God's story.

Of course, some people have a clear sense of their own story. But even they can be enriched when they hear the stories of others. In our relationship with others, we discover new meaning in our lives. Furthermore, in the telling of our stories to others, we are affirmed in who we are.

Pilgrimage

As Christians we have come to understand that our stories are not random. In fact, to become a follower of Jesus is to seek to walk in his way. This Way is not some vague pathway; it is a well-marked road; first walked by Jesus, the author and pioneer of our faith; then walked by the Twelve and others in the first century; and later walked by innumerable men and women through the centuries: people from different ages, different races, different cultures. We have testimonies left by our forebears that tell us of the character of the Way. To be a Christian is to be a pilgrim; it is to be on a journey. Our story becomes the story of our pilgrimage.

When we understand that we are part of a great and glorious company who are called the people of God, we have a new frame of reference for interpreting our lives. Now the question becomes: are we walking in the way that leads to conformity with the life of Jesus? Are we living in the way that brings wholeness to us? Is this wholeness God's wholeness? After all, as our Creator, God knows best how we are meant to function. As our loving Parent, God knows our destiny, our place in the eternal scheme of things. And in finding our divinely-ordained niche, we find purpose and meaning in life.

Community

Through our stories we come into community with others. This is another theme running through these books: the nature and process of community. It is my contention that the root of community is found in sharing our stories with one another. It is very difficult to dislike or disdain someone whose story you have heard. Furthermore, as we listen to a story we make links, we reach out, we connect with one another. This is especially true when we share a commitment to a common story.

The uniqueness of Christian community is found in the fact that we try to connect our stories with God's story; that we assess our stories on the basis of what we read in the Bible; that we relate to others who are walking in Jesus' way and are his people here and now.

It is true that the Christian way was never meant to be a solitary way. We walk our pilgrimage in the company of others who help us in this journey (just as we help others). We are family. We are brothers and sisters. So it is not surprising that we would learn spiritual disciplines in the company of others. In this day and age when time is in such short supply for so many of us, it is unlikely that we will have the desire (much less the knowledge) to pursue spiritual disciplines on our own. We need a small group of like-minded pilgrims with whom we learn, who hold us accountable (as we hold them accountable), and who support us in our journey.

Disciplines

The spiritual disciplines are simply ways of living that seek to conform us with the image of Christ. By practicing these disciplines, we train ourselves to respond in Christian ways to events in our life. In particular, the spiritual disciplines keep us alert to the presence of God. God is always active. This is God's nature. But for many people, the voice of God is no more than a mere whisper heard only in crisis (if at all). Continued inattention to the presence of God ongoing decisions that lead us away from God decrease our awareness of our God-given spiritual natures. The spiritual disciplines are a way of learning to hear again, a way to respond positively to God.

For those who call themselves Christians, the immediacy of God can be lost in the routine. Worship, Bible study, fellowship, and even prayer become an end in themselves, not a path to the presence of God. God's voice is muted. Or it is confused with unexamined cultural or personal baggage. It becomes hard to hear God clearly or to know Him intimately. In this case, the spiritual disciplines become a way to sort out the "voices" that would demand our attention and to notice the Voice. They also enable us to stay in touch with God and to develop our spiritual lives.

This series focuses on five disciplines:
- *The Discipline of Journaling:* This is a way of noticing and processing both the unfolding of our lives in the present and the uncovering of our past.

- *The Discipline of Spiritual Autobiography:* This work enables us to know our unique story and thus gives us a perspective from which to make future decisions. Telling our stories to others connects us the Christian community in deep and sustaining ways. Furthermore, as we learn the discipline of noticing God, we close, little by little, the gap between the spiritual and the temporal in our lives.

- *The Discipline of Bible Reflection:* which helps us understand the meaning of our stories. As we learn to reflect on Scripture we develop a way of knowing that puts us in touch with God's wisdom. It is a way of hearing God. The discipline of Bible reflection includes Bible study but goes beyond it in significant ways.

- *The Discipline of Prayer:* This puts us to directly in touch with God. There is not one way of prayer (though many people use only one prayer style); there are many ways. How we pray relates to our personality type; what our needs are at any given point; where we are in our spiritual pilgrimage. We need to enlarge our prayer vocabulary.

- *The Discipline of Repentance and Faith:* This gives us a way of changing. Various activities are included in this discipline: confession, forgiveness, acceptance of grace; strong trust in God. As we practice this discipline, we bring intentionality to our growth as Christians.

The Series of Books

There are five books in the SPIRITUAL DISCIPLINES series. Each helps us in uncovering, sharing, understanding, growing, and changing our stories. While it is not necessary to work through each book in sequence (each is free-standing and can be used on its own), the series moves in a logical progression:

Book One: *Spiritual Journaling: Recording Your Journey Toward God.* Through journaling we uncover and process the data of our spiritual pilgrimage as well as stay in touch with our unfolding story.

Book Two: *Spiritual Storytelling: Discovering and Sharing Your Spiritual Autobiography.* A spiritual autobiography describes our pilgrimage with God over time. The process of writing a spiritual autobiography is useful; telling our story to others deepens its value.

Book Three: *Contemplative Bible Reading: Experiencing God Through Scripture.* Our stories need to be interpreted in light of God's story. Through crucial an ancient process of biblical meditation (*lectio divina*), we encounter the crucial stories of the Bible through which we learn the meaning of our stories.

Book Four: *Meditative Prayer: Entering God's Presence.* Next we need to offer our stories to God. We can use various ways of praying as we seek both to understand and to deal with our stories in a helpful way.

Book Five: *Spiritual Transformation: Taking on the Character of Christ.* Ultimately the goal of our pilgrimage is to be conformed to the image of Christ. The twin acts of repentance and faith provide the way of transformation.

The Art of Leadership: Brief Reflections on How to Lead a Small Group

It's not difficult to be a small group leader. All you need is:
- The willingness to do so;
- The commitment to read through all of the materials prior to the session;
- The sensitivity to others that will allow you to guide the discussion without dominating it;
- The willingness to be used by God as a small group leader.

Here are some basic small group principles that will help you do your job:

- **Ask the questions:** Your role is to ask the questions. Let group members respond.

- **Guide the discussion:** Ask follow-up questions (or make comments) that draw others into the discussion and keep the discussion going. For example:
  ▶ "John, how would you answer the question?"
  ▶ "Anybody else have any insights into this question?"

- **Start and stop on time:** If you don't, people may be hesitant to come again since they never know when they will get home.

- **Stick to the time allotted to each section:** There is always more that can be said in response to any question. It's your job to make sure that the discussion keeps moving from question to question. Remember: it's better to cut off discussion when it's going well than to let it go on until it dies out.

- **Model answers to questions:** Whenever you ask a question to which everyone is expected to respond (for example, a "Stories" question as opposed to a Bible study question), you, as leader, should be the first person to respond. In this way you model the right length—and appropriate level—of response.

- **Understand the intention of different kinds of questions:**
  ▶ *Experience questions:* The aim is to cause people to recall past experiences and share these memories with the group. There are no right or wrong answers to these questions. They facilitate the group process by getting people to share their stories and to think about the topic.
  ▶ *Forced-choice questions:* Certain questions will be followed by a series of suggested answers (with check-boxes). Generally, there is no "correct" answer. Options aid group members and guide their responses.
  ▶ *Analysis questions:* These force the group to notice what the Bible text says and to explore it for meaning.
  ▶ *Application questions:* These help the group make connections between the meaning of the text and their own lives.

▶ *Questions with multiple parts:* Sometimes a question is asked and then various aspects of it are listed below. Ask the group members to answer each of the sub-questions. Their answers, taken together, will answer the initial question.

- **Introduce each section:** This may involve a brief overview of the focus, purpose, and topic of the new section and instructions on how to do the exercise.

- **Comments:** Occasionally bring into the discussion some useful information from your own study. Keep your comments brief. Don't allow yourself to become the "expert" to whom everyone turns for "the right answer." Invite comments from others.

Here are some insights into how the small group discussion is structured in this book:

- **There are five parts to each small group session and each has a different aim:**
  ▶ *Stories:* The purpose of this section is to: help people move from the worries and concerns (which they brought with them to the small group) to the topic itself; start people thinking about the topic in terms of their own experiences; start discussion among group members; encourage people to tell their stories to each other so they get to know one another.

  ▶ *Discuss:* The purpose of this section is to: discuss the process of preparing and presenting a spiritual autobiography; develop clear expectations for each person when it comes to preparing and presenting their stories; motivate and encourage one another in preparation; plan together for the presentation of spiritual autobiographies.

  ▶ *Study:* The purpose of this section is to do a Bible study together which involves: a brief introduction to the text; reading the text; working through the questions in order to understand what the text is saying and how it applies to each person; referring to the Bible Study Notes that provide the background to the text.

  ▶ *Pray:* The purpose of this section is to: end the session with prayer related to the issues discussed; commit the process of spiritual autobiography to God.

  ▶ Homework: The purpose of this section is to guide group members in the preparation of a spiritual autobiography.

Here is the process you (as small group leader) should follow in each of the five Bible study sessions:

- **Begin each new session by welcoming everyone.**
  ▶ Open in prayer. Your prayer does not need to be long or complex. You can write it out beforehand. In your prayer, thank God for his presence. Ask him to guide the group into new wisdom, and to give each person the courage to respond to the text. You do not have to be the one who always opens in prayer. You can ask others to pray. It is usually a good idea to ask beforehand if a person is willing to pray aloud.

▶Introduce the topic: Take no more than one minute to do this. Simply refer to the three sections in the beginning of each chapter.
- *Preparing for Sharing:* This describes the intention of the *Discuss* section. This portion of the small group session looks forward to the time when the sharing of spiritual autobiographies occurs.
- *Bible Study Theme:* This describes the focus of the text and its connection to the process of spiritual autobiography.
- *Session Aims:* The goals of the session are Summarized.

- **Move to the *Stories* exercise.**
  ▶Read aloud the brief introduction (when there is one) or simply introduce the theme of the exercise.
  ▶Give people a minute to read over the questions and think about their answers.
  ▶Then, as leader, begin the sharing by giving your answer to the first question.
  - Remember, there are no "right" answers, only personal stories or preferences.
  - Laughter is great medicine. These questions are seldom serious and invite funny stories (often from childhood).
  ▶Move to the person on your right and ask him or her to respond. Go around the circle so each person has a chance to respond to the question.
  ▶Move to question two and do the same thing.
  ▶Finish up with question three.
  ▶Watch the time carefully so everyone has a chance to respond.
  - Don't worry if you do not get through all three questions, as long as people have started sharing. After a few sessions you will know how many questions you can get through with your group. You may need to pre-select one or two questions to use for this sharing time.
  ▶Remember that even though this is lighthearted sharing, you are discussing the topic of the Bible study. Remind people of the theme of the subject.

- **Move to the second section of the small group session: *Discuss.***
  ▶Identify the issue or issues of that session's discussion.
  ▶If there is a reference to material in the manual, ask people to turn to it and read it over quickly.
  ▶If there are tasks to be performed (such as developing a schedule for sharing spiritual autobiographies), be sure to complete it.
  ▶Be encouraging as you discuss the joys and trials of preparing a spiritual autobiography.
  ▶Keep in mind that the essence of this small group is sharing spiritual autobiographies. This is why you are meeting. Use this time to prepare for this.

- **Move to the third section of the small group: *Study***
  ▶Introduce the Bible passage by reading aloud (or summarizing in your own words) the introduction to this section.
  ▶Read the Bible passage (or invite someone else to read it).
  ▶Give the group a few minutes to read over the passage, read through the questions (and think about the answers), and to consult the *Bible Study Notes.*

▶ Ask question one; get responses from several people.

▶ When you feel that the question has been sufficiently discussed, move to the next question.

- In this section, some of the initial questions are fact-oriented. There are specific answers to them. Subsequent questions will be more open-ended and will invite discussion.
- Spend only a little time on the fact questions. They encourage people to notice carefully what the text says. But the heart of the study is found in the discussion related to the meaning and the application of the text.
- If you spend too much time on fact questions, it can become just another "boring Bible study." Keep up the pace.
- Feel free to omit some of the fact questions if time is a problem.
- Notice that each question set begins with a title that defines the focus of that group of questions. This helps you understand the direction of the questions. Sometimes you may want to ask only one question with respect to the issue.

▶ Work through all of the questions:

- Be sure you have thought about the questions beforehand so that you recognize the important questions that need more time.

▶ If you have time, use the optional question. These quotations invite discussion and personal sharing that will fill the remaining time. You may decide to skip some questions and end with the optional question.

▶ Remember: your aim in the Bible study is to help the group understand better the nature of a spiritual pilgrimage so that they have insight into their own pilgrimage and will find it easier to write their spiritual autobiography.

- **Conclude the small group session.**

  ▶ End with prayer together. The topics of prayer are defined. Develop a style of prayer which fits your group. This may be:

  - *Free prayer:* people are asked to pray as they feel led about the topics.
  - *Conversational prayer:* one person begins praying about a topic in a sentence or two, and then a second person joins the conversation and prays a few more sentences, and so on until a person begins to pray about the next topic.
  - *Liturgical prayer:* give people time to write down a short prayer which they will read during the prayer time.
  - *Leader prayer:* the leader or someone who has volunteered prays for the whole group.
  - *Silent prayer:* after the allotted time, the leader closes with a brief spoken prayer.

  ▶ Discuss the *Homework* for the coming week:

  - Encourage people to review the *Bible Study Notes* (if they have not had time to do so during the small group).
  - Encourage people in their work on their spiritual autobiographies.

- Serve coffee, tea, soft drinks, etc. This will give people a chance to talk informally. There is often very good conversation following a small group session, as people hash over the evening's discussion.

Small Group Leader's Guide: Notes on Each Session

Starting a Small Group for Spiritual Storytelling

If you are the small group leader, it is important for you to read carefully the section entitled *The Art of Leadership: Brief Reflections on How to Lead a Small Group.* This will help you lead your small group, and you will understand how this particular small group series has been structured. It will also give you some ideas as to how you can adapt the material to fit the needs of your group. Before each session, go over the notes for that session (see below). These will focus on the specific materials in each session.

The Preparatory Bible Studies

There are two ways to conduct this small group program.
- ▶ *Full Option:* Follow the program as outlined in the book, that is:
  - Do the five Bible studies on the pilgrimage of Abraham and cover the various organizational details. During these five weeks, group members will work on their own to prepare their spiritual autobiography. This will involve reading Parts II and III of the Study Guide individually and then writing their spiritual autobiographies (5 weeks).
  - Follow the Bible studies with as many small group sessions as necessary so that each person in the group can present their spiritual autobiography (5 to 13 weeks).
  - Conclude with the Celebration (Small Group Session Seven) (1 week).
- ▶ *Shortened Option:* In this case, you will skip the Bible studies and go straight to the presentation of spiritual autobiographies. However, you will need at least two organizational meetings prior to the presentation of the first spiritual autobiography. These two meetings are necessary in order for the group to become familiar with one another (it is hard to present an honest spiritual autobiography to a group of strangers). And it is important to create a good structure within which to present the stories. In these two organizational meetings:
  - Session 1: Use the *Stories* ("Biographies"), *Discuss* (talk about how to write a spiritual autobiography), and *Pray* sections from Small Group Session One. In addition, do the *Discuss* section in Small Group Session Two (create a covenant). Make sure you have a volunteer who will present their spiritual autobiography in week 3.
  - Session 2: Use the *Stories* and *Pray* sections from Small Group Session Two ("Family Stories"), the *Discuss* section (sharing a spiritual autobiography and making a calendar for sharing) from Small Group Session Three, and the *Discuss* section (starting spiritual autobiography sessions) from Small Group Session Five.
  - Session 3 and following: For each subsequent week, allow one person to present his or her spiritual autobiography. If you are really

pressed for time, you can expand these sessions to two hours and do two spiritual autobiographies per session. However, experience shows that the best sessions are limited to one person per week. You may or may not want to do the final Celebration session (7). However, if you skip that session, spend some time deciding on what the small group will do next (see the *What's Next* section) at the end of the final spiritual autobiography (pages 39–40).

Session One: Pilgrimage

▶ **The special character of Session One:** The first session is very important. People who attend will be deciding whether they want to be a part of the group. So your aim as small group leader is to:
- Create excitement about this small group (so each person will want to continue);
- Give people an overview of the series (so they know where they are headed);
- Begin to build relationships (so that a sense of community starts to develop);
- Encourage people to commit to the small group (so everyone will return next week, and perhaps bring a friend!).

▶ **Potluck:** A good way to launch the first session of any small group is by eating together prior to the session. Sharing a meal draws people together and breaks down barriers between them.
- Ask everyone to bring along one dish for the supper. This makes it easy to have a meal for twelve! Or if you feel ambitious, you might want to invite everyone to dinner at your place. What you serve doesn't need to be elaborate. Conversation (not feasting) is the intention of the get-together.
- The aim of the meal is to get to know one another in this informal setting. Structure the meal in such a way that a lot of conversation takes place.
- Following the meal, be sure to complete the first session (and not just talk about what you are going to do when the group starts). Your aim is to give everyone the experience of what it would mean to be a part of this small group.

▶ Introduction to the Session
- **Welcome:** Greet people and let them know you're glad that they've come, and that you look forward to being with them for the next few weeks.
- **Prayer:** Pray briefly, thanking God for this group and asking Him to guide your deliberations and sharing today. Ask God to guide you in discovering the power of a spiritual autobiography in developing your spiritual lives and that you will all learn the discipline of noticing His presence.
- **Group Process:** Describe how the small group will function and what it will study. Discuss, specifically:
  ▶ **Series Theme:** The aim is to prepare and present a spiritual autobiography.
  ▶ **Group Experience:** Describe how the five Bible studies will func-

tion, and then how each spiritual autobiography will be presented and discussed.

▶ **Group Details:** Discuss where you will meet, when, and how long each session will last.

▶ **Group Aims:** The hope is that each person's spiritual growth will be enhanced by writing and presenting a spiritual autobiography, and by learning the spiritual discipline of noticing God.

▶ Do Session One, using the material in the book and following the outline for how to do a Bible study in *The Art of Leadership* section. Be alert to the following issues:

• *Stories:* The aim of this session is to start the process of group building by sharing brief stories and information. The theme of the exercise is "Biographies" and is intended to provoke thinking about spiritual autobiography. Do not let question 3 take much time. When you (as leader) answer this question, do so in a few sentences as a model for the others. Remember that this issue will be covered thoroughly as you each present your spiritual autobiographies.

• *Discuss:* Do not spend a lot of time reading the material on preparing a spiritual autobiography. Just glance at it. This material should be read individually between small group sessions. The aim of this discussion is to encourage people to think about writing their spiritual autobiography.

• *Study:* Keep in mind constantly that the aim of this Bible study (and those that follow) is to expand each member's understanding of spiritual pilgrimage, and to make it easier to write a spiritual autobiography. Keep this focus during each session.

  ▶ In general terms, the first two sets of questions focus on the Hebrews 11–12 text, while the last two sets of questions focus on the application of the material to each person's life.

  ▶ Question 2 is an example of a fact-oriented question that can (and should) be answered quickly.

  ▶ Notice that the themes of movement and goal in pilgrimage are emphasized.

  ▶ Try the optional question. This invites more of an unstructured discussion. If it works well with your group, you may want to leave time in each of the following sessions for this exercise.

• *Group Invitation:* If your first session is a "trial meeting," invite everyone to return next week. If you have room in the small group (i.e., there are less than twelve people), encourage members to invite their friends. After week two, new people cannot join the group, since each time a new person comes it is necessary to rebuild the sense of community.

Session Two: Call and Blessing

▶ *Introduction to the Session:* Welcome new people and let them know you're glad that they have come and that you look forward to your time together. As you did last week, open in prayer and quickly explain the aims of the session.

▶ Do Session Two, using the material in the book and following the outline for how to do a Bible study in *The Art of Leadership* section. Be alert to the following issues:
  • *Discuss:* It is especially important in a small group where spiritual autobiographies will be shared that a clear covenant is developed. This gives group members confidence that what they share will be well received and kept within the group.
  • *Study:* Continue to distinguish between questions that need little time to answer and those that invite reflection and discussion.

Session Three: Encounters

▶ Do Session Three, using the material in the book and following the outline for how to do a Bible study in *The Art of Leadership* section. Be alert to the following issue:
  • *Study:* This is a longer passage than you have studied together so far. You may want to ask the group to read it silently, since this will be quicker. Also, no one will have to pronounce the names in verses 19–21!

Session Four: Relationships

▶ Do Session Four, using the material in the book and following the outline for how to do a Bible study in *The Art of Leadership* section. Be alert to the following issues:
  • *Discuss:* The issue here will be to encourage one another in the writing process. Some people may be having difficulties.
  • *Study:* Now you have two passages to work through, not one. You will have to be careful not to spend too much time on only one passage. Give each equal weight. Keep the focus clearly in mind as you guide the discussion. Be sure to get to question 3. This will generate good discussion, especially since the group has been thinking about these things as they write their spiritual autobiographies.

Session Five: Testing

▶ Do Session Five, using the material in the book and following the outline for how to do a Bible study in *The Art of Leadership* section. Be alert to the following issue:
  • *Discuss:* Get ready for the first spiritual autobiography session next week. Take whatever time you need so that Session Six will run smoothly.

Session Six: Spiritual Autobiography

▶ You have now come to why this group is meeting: to hear each other's spiritual autobiographies. It is important that the session leader do everything possible to facilitate a good session. Be clear about who does what, and watch the time carefully.

Final Session: Celebration

▶ It is important to bring closure to every small group, and especially to one like this that has shared deeply with one another.

Bible Study Notes

Chapter One Bible Study Notes

Setting: Hebrews 11 is a celebration of the character of faith, expressed through vivid language and through the stories of saints of old. Based on these examples, there is a call in Hebrews 12 for steadfast endurance in the face of hostility on the part of the people of faith. We look at one story in this catalog of faith, that of Abraham. The journey of Abraham to the land of Canaan was a powerful metaphor for the people of Israel. It became the image of what God called them to as a nation: obedient pilgrimage to the promised land. The phrase, "the promised land," is used in two senses: in the immediate sense, the promised land is Palestine (which eventually became the home of the Jewish people); in the ultimate sense, it is the New Jerusalem (the heavenly home of all of God's people).

faith: The word "faith" is used some twenty-four times in Hebrews 11. The life of faith is based on a deep belief and trust in God and His promises. This faith is characterized by "firmness, reliability, and steadfastness . . . . What these attested witnesses affirm is the reliability of God, who is faithful to his promise" (Lane).

By faith: This phrase is used to introduce a number of examples of faith—this is the first. What follows in Hebrews 11 is a catalog of people and events, presented in chronological order, that illustrate the nature of faith as it is defined in the first verse. Here the example is of our conviction (though we could never know it directly) that God created the physical world by his word of command.

what we do not see: The literal translation is: "faith is . . . the conviction of things not seen." Faith is conviction: a deep trust in God. Faith is hope: a trust that what God has declared to be so is true even though it is yet unseen.

Abraham: Abraham is the towering figure of the OT, without whom there would have been no OT story at all. More than twelve chapters of Genesis are used to tell his story. He is called the "friend of God" (2 Chronicle 20:7; Isaiah 41:8; James 2:23). Scripture writers frequently refer to "the God of Abraham" when describing the God of Israel. In the NT he is referred to in all four Gospels and Acts, as well as in five epistles (Romans, Galatians, Hebrews, James, and 1 Peter), where he is often used as an illustration concerning faith. It is through Abraham that God has chosen to bless all of humanity. Abraham is considered the "father of all who believe" (Romans 4:11); the model of what a life of faith is all about. The story of Abraham is told in Genesis 11:27–25:11.

obeyed: Faith produces action. God called; Abraham obeyed.

to a place: This was Canaan, the promised land. Canaan is an early name for Palestine. Before the coming of the Jewish people, it was occupied by the Canaanites.

went: Abraham lived in the center of the then-civilized world. Ur of the Chaldeans (probably in southern Iraq) had a sophisticated culture. King Ur-Nammu, who published an ancient code of law, may well have ruled during this era. Abraham left all of this in order to travel into the wilderness.

he did not know where he was going: Abraham's faith prompted him to leave on this journey even though he had no clear idea where it would take him. What he did know was that God had called him to this journey, so he was willing to undertake it—even though what was promised was nowhere in sight.

he lived in tents: Abraham was a nomad, not staying long in any place as he moved toward the Promised Land.

Isaac and Jacob: Abraham's son and grandson, through whom the line of descent would run and from whom the nation of Israel would emerge.

looking forward to the city: It is hope that makes faith possible: Abraham's strong sense that God had prepared a place for him made it possible for Abraham to undertake his journey. It is faith that empowers hope: the deep trust Abraham had in God gave him assurance that there was actually a city waiting for him. Faith and hope work together: faith is the attitude of trust that keeps us going; hope is the confidence that what we have believed is real and not simply wishful thinking. In other words, faith has a forward-looking character to it. Faith gives what we hope for (based on God's promise) a substantial reality in the here and now even though, in fact, it will only be realized in the future.

run with perseverance: This is the key response that the writer is urging in us: endurance; hanging in there when things get tough for us as people of faith.

race: The metaphor of an athletic contest is used.

fix our eyes on Jesus: Jesus is our model; he is our example. We see in him the twin attributes of faithfulness and endurance that the writer of Hebrews urges us to emulate. His death on the cross is "the supreme example of persevering faith" (Lane).

Chapter Two Bible Study Notes

Abram: This was Abraham's original name. It means "exalted father."

The Lord had said to Abram: Why God chose Abraham for this task is not explained, only the nature of his call is described. This was a sovereign act of God, not something Abraham deserved or earned.

Leave your country: Abram grew up in Ur, a Chaldean city in the Fertile Crescent where ancient civilizations flourished. Ur was an important commercial center located on the Euphrates River near the Persian Gulf. The people had an understanding of mathematics and astronomy, and a written language that they used to record their ideas and culture on clay tablets (which have been excavated by archaeologists). At the center of the city was a large ziggurat (temple) where the moon god Nanna was worshiped. Terah, Abraham's father, set out for Canaan but only traveled as far as Haran, in northern Mesopotamia.

leave your people and your father's household: This was a far more serious undertaking in Abraham's day than in our own. It was one's tribe, and especially one's father, who provided protection and a place where you were known and accepted. To leave was to turn your back on this entire support system with nothing to replace it.

Canaan: God calls Abraham and his family to leave one of the major centers of the known world and travel hundreds of miles to a rural outpost on the eastern coast of the Mediterranean Sea.

seventy-five years old: Abraham was not a young man when he began this journey. Scripture, in this condensed account, only records that Abraham left when God called. But surely it must not have been easy: to leave this sophisticated urban center and journey to who knows where because God called (How did Abraham know the one true God in the midst of the many gods of Ur and Haran?) must have been exceedingly difficult. The sheer logistics of moving a large family were formidable.

Blessing: To bless someone is to convey something of yourself to that person: your energy and your character. It is to commission a person to the task demanded of him or her. To be blessed is to be empowered. It is to be affirmed. It is to be given a future (see Genesis 27:27–29; 48:15–16) In the OT, God's blessing is frequently seen in such things as prosperity, long life, children, wealth, peace, good harvests (Genesis 24:35–36; Leviticus 26:4–13; Deuteronomy 28:3–15). Our modern equivalent of "blessing" is "good luck" or "success," with the difference being that the OT insists that it is God (and not "fate" or "chance" or even "hard work") that brings blessing. "God alone is the source of all good fortune" (Wenham). Abraham will become a source of blessing to others—in fact, to all the families on earth.

I will bless you: The key fact about Abraham is that he has no heir. His wife, Sarai, is barren (Genesis 11:30). To be without an heir is to have no future. His line has come to an end. It is this man with no heir whom God has chosen to launch a new people; a nation through whom God will make himself known to the whole world. Thus Abraham's blessing is not from his father (whom he is called to leave) or from having a son (who would ensure a future); it is from God who gives him, unexpectedly, a future.

A great nation: Abraham is promised four things: a nation, greatness, God's protection, and God's blessing. Abraham is promised that his descendant will blossom into a genuine nation (as opposed to an extended family or even a large clan). A nation implies a large population that lives in an extended geographical area and is united by language and government.

make your name great: To be the father of a nation would mean that people would look back to Abraham with respect, as indeed is true of the nation of Israel.

Chapter Three Bible Study Notes

a vision: a well-recognized mode of revelation whereby a human being encounters God (or some other supernatural being). In this vision Abraham is assured of both protection and reward.

Do not be afraid: To encounter the living God is an awesome experience. Our natural response is fear. God seeks to calm Abraham; to assure him that his power will not destroy.

reward: The word means a gift given, not a wage earned. The gift of God comes to those who trust, but the trust (or faith) is not the cause of the reward. God gives the gift freely. This is an essential biblical perspective.

But Abraham said: Rather than thanking or praising God, Abraham protests. He still has the same problem that he has always had: no child. Abraham is not passive before God. He is quite willing to urge God to solve his problem so he can receive the reward which God has promised.

heir: This is still the issue. When Abraham and Sarah left Haran they were a childless couple, but they left with the promise that they would have an heir from whom a great nation would spring (see Genesis 12:2, 7; 13:16). It is years later and there is still no heir. Sarah continues to be barren and is likely to remain so at her advanced age.

Eliezer of Damascus: According to some tablets found in Northern Mesopotamia (where Haran was located), a childless couple could adopt a son who would be their heir. This is apparently what they have done (or will do) with Eliezer of Damascus. However, these tablets also indicate that should they bear a son, that child would become the heir (though he would share some of his inheritance with the previously adopted child).

the word of the Lord: After Abraham's double protest, God responds with a double promise. First there is the word: God reiterates what he promised in the past.

Look: Next comes the sign: the star-filled sky. The same God who can make the stars can give a son.

Abram believed: He moves from disbelief (or at least, from doubt) to belief; he moves from protest to confession; he goes from despair to hope. Abraham repented (i.e., he changed his mind about his former concerns). Once again he is sure of God and is hopeful about the future. It is now the future that captivates him (and what God will do), not the past which enslaves him (because of what he does not have).

credited to him as righteousness: Usually when righteousness is mentioned in the OT, it refers to actions which are approved by God. What is in view here is how Abraham has done. His faith counts as righteousness. But it is not his faith (or belief) that brings about this declaration. His faith is simply a response to God. However, as the story of Abraham later shows, faith results in righteous action (18:19). In legal terms, a righteous person is one who is acquitted. So in spiritual terms, the righteous are acquitted by God on the Day of Judgment and are therefore saved. The great declaration in verse 6 is important to NT writers. Paul quotes it twice (Romans 4:3; Galatians 3:6) and James once (James 2:23).

heifer, etc.: Animals that are allowed to be offered for sacrifice.

cut them in two: The covenant ritual is similar to what is found in Jeremiah 34:18.

verses 13–16: A prophecy of the bondage in Egypt and the subsequent exodus. The promise of God to Abraham has both immediate and far-reaching consequences. Abraham will have his long-delayed son, but the forming of the great nation and living in the land will take generations to accomplish. However, Abraham can go to his death at the end of his long life knowing that the full promise will be fulfilled.

Amorites: The inhabitants of Canaan.

smoking fire pot: A large earthenware jar that was used as an oven for baking. Smoke and fire are symbols of the presence of God. It is God who moves among the sacrifice.

covenant: Typically, covenants are binding agreements that impose obligations on both parties. But here the covenant is one-sided. God promises land to Abraham with no requirement on Abraham's part. This is an act of sheer grace. As with the promise in verses 4–5, all Abraham has to do is trust God.

Chapter Four Bible Study Notes

Genesis 16

maidservant: the companion and helper of a rich woman.

Abraham agreed: Having heard and accepted God's promise to give him a son (in Genesis 15), Abraham now seems to forget. He capitulates to Sarah's plan to solve the problem of her childlessness.

I can build a family through her: The custom of surrogate motherhood was common in this era. Though this was a normal and respectable solution to childlessness, it was not a wise solution (as the passage shows).

ten years: The vividness of Abraham's experience with God has faded. God's promise of an heir has not yet been fulfilled. So Abraham allows Sarah to take matters into her own hands. He agrees to solve the problem in her way.

his wife: Polygamy was common.

despise her mistress: In this unfortunate triangle, all three characters respond in less than positive ways. Hagar begins to look down on Sarah, probably resenting Sarah's role as the first wife when Hagar is the one who will bear the heir.

you are responsible: Sarah, in turn, blames Abraham (even though it was her plan).

Do with her whatever: Abraham, for his part, refuses to accept any responsibility (even though Hagar is now his wife and he should protect her and her child).

mistreated: Literally, humiliated. Sarah is jealous of Hagar and responds unfairly and unjustly to her. Since she literally owns her, she has great power to make her life miserable.

Genesis 20

"She is my sister": This is the second time that Abraham has claimed Sarah is his sister and let a powerful man take her into his royal harem (see Genesis 12:10–20)!

God came to Abimelech in a dream: Even though it was Abraham's cowardice that created this situation, God protects him and Sarah through a dream in which God warns Abimelech of the true situation. Abraham may be unfaithful, but God is faithful and protects the bearers of the promise. Note too that God communicates with the foreigner, Abimelech, and that Abimelech clearly recognizes who is speaking to him in the dream. God did not exclusively speak to Abraham. God is active throughout the world.

you are as good as dead . . . she is a married woman: That adultery merited death was widely accepted in the ancient world (Wenham).

clear conscience: Abimelech claims that he has kept his integrity in all of this.

I did not let you touch her: Just before the story of Isaac's birth (in Genesis 21), it is important that there be no question as to who the father of Isaac is.

verses 11–13: Abraham offers a series of weak excuses for his behavior.

they will kill me because of my wife: Abraham's fear, now as before (Genesis 12:12–13), is that he will be harmed (or killed) because the ruler will want Sarah for his harem. Abraham is willing to allow Abimelech to sleep with her if it will save him.

no fear of God in this place: Abraham excuses himself by charging that Abimelech does not fear God when, in fact, Abimelech both fears and obeys God (while Abraham, as this story shows, fears many things other than God).

she really is my sister: Abraham was not actually lying. What he said was, in fact, true. However, he failed to reveal the full situation: namely, that they were also married. Such marriages between close relatives was later banned by the Law of Moses.

verses 14-15: There is an irony here—Abraham emerges from his fearfulness and faithlessness with enhanced wealth and power. Abraham's position (as the chosen one to bless the nations) was not due to his worthiness (which he again fails to display), but because God will faithfully fulfill his promises.

Chapter Five Bible Study Notes

Setting: Chapter 21 tells the story of Isaac's birth. Finally, after years of waiting and against all the odds, Sarah becomes pregnant and Isaac is born. At last there is an heir. Abraham's line will continue. The promise will be fulfilled. A great nation will emerge. But in chapter 22, all of this changes. God's great promise is put in peril by God's dark command.

Why was Abraham put to such an awful test? We cannot ever know. Perhaps it is because God knew the outcome. He knew that over the years Abraham had developed such a deep and unwavering trust that he would be able both to believe the promise and follow the command. Likewise, perhaps Abraham had to undergo a radical testing because with great calling (and few have had a greater calling—to father a people through which God would bless the whole world) comes great testing (and Abraham is found faithful). Perhaps, also, God needed to show the world that he is a God of life, and that the only sacrifice he will ever ask is of himself and not us.

Out of this experience the world learned that the God of Abraham was not like the other gods. He did not command the killing of a child. Later in the history of Israel (during the time of Moses), this prohibition against killing is included in the Ten Commandments. Likewise, Abraham and Isaac's experience prepared us to understand the later sacrifice of a son: God's own Son died on a cross for the sake of all humanity (Romans 8:31–32).

God tested Abraham: The point of the story is made clear: not whether Isaac will be killed, but whether Abraham can stand up to this test. Testing shows what is in the heart of a person. But Abraham does not know this is a test. He must go through this awful time when he is torn between his love for his son and his love for God; between his joy that God has given him an heir and his horror that his heir will die; between his faith in God's promise and his willingness to obey God's command. God uses this experience to free Abraham from the assumptions of his culture—that killing a child pleases God.

Take: In fact, the better translation is "Please take." This is a rare form of divine command that softens the blow to Abraham and hints at the fact that God knows how very difficult this will be for Abraham to hear (much less do).

go: When God called Abraham to leave his homeland, clan, and family in chapter 12, the difficulty of that command was lessened by the promise of a new home and a great nation. But here there is no promise, no incentive—only command.

Sacrifice him: A horrific command if ever there was one. It is hard to imagine any father sacrificing his son, but this was especially difficult in Abraham's case. Not only did he love Isaac deeply ("Isaac whom you love"), but Isaac was a miracle child born well beyond the childbearing years of both of his parents. Isaac was also a son of promise—the heir ("your only son") given by God, the one who would fulfill God's great promises to Abraham. Herein lies the tension. It is through Isaac that God's promises will be fulfilled (21:12). Isaac is the very point of the pilgrimage: a childless couple bear a son who will bring blessing. But if Isaac dies, they become childless again and the entire pilgrimage will have been for nothing. Abraham is called upon to believe and to obey even though these two elements are in sharp contradiction.

burnt offering: In ancient times this was a way of worship; a way to appease the gods, a way of forgiveness.

On the third day: This was not a test that would soon be over. Imagine the agony of Abraham during these days: the wondering, the fear, the despair, the temptation to turn aside.

we will come back to you: Did Abraham say this to the two servants because he didn't want to reveal what he had been asked to do? Or did he know in his heart of hearts that somehow God would save his son?

God himself will provide the sacrifice: It is impossible to know how Abraham imagined that God would fulfill his promise of a great nation through Isaac while commanding Abraham to kill him. Probably the answer lay in this response to Isaac's question. This was an answer to quell Isaac's question (and fears?), but it was probably also the answer to Abraham's fear, though he did not know it yet. "Abraham knows beyond understanding that God will find a way to bring life even in this scenario of death. That is the faith of Abraham" (Brueggemann).

Do not lay a hand on the boy: The God who tests is the God who provides. He is the God who does not demand a child as a sacrifice.

fear God: To fear God is a common OT expression and means to honor God, by worship and by a righteous life (Job 1:1; 8:2–3).

a ram caught by his horns: God provides the animal to take Isaac's place. There is a strong parallel here to Jesus, God's own Son, who died in our place.

Summary: The story of Abraham and Isaac is very important to the writers of the NT. It prepares us to understand the death of Jesus. Whereas God would not ask Abraham to sacrifice his only son, God gives up Jesus, his only Son, to die on the cross. Echoes of Genesis 22:12 ("... you have not withheld from me your son, your only son") are found in John 3:16 "For God so loved the world that he gave his only Son . . . ." Paul says, "If God is for us, who is against us? He who did not spare his own Son but gave him up for us. . . " (Romans 8:31–32). John the Baptist cries out, "Behold the Lamb of God, who takes away the sin of the world!" pointing to the meaning of Jesus' sacrifice. Furthermore, in his baptism, Jesus is, like Isaac, called "the beloved son." In Jesus we find the tension between testing and providing most clearly illustrated. Crucifixion is the ultimate test. Resurrection is the ultimate provision.

A Select Bibliography

Books about Spiritual Autobiography

Baldwin, Christina. *Life's Companion: Journal Writing as a Spiritual Quest.* New York: Bantam Books, 1990.

Keen, Sam and Anne Valley-Fox. *Your Mythic Journey: Finding Meaning in Your Life Through Writing and Storytelling.* Los Angeles: Jeremy P. Tarcher, Inc. 1973, 1989.

McClendon, James W. *Biography as Theology: How Life Stories Can Remake Today's Theology.* Philadelphia: Trinity Press International, 1974, 1990.

Peace, Richard. *Pilgrimage: A Handbook on Christian Growth.* Grand Rapids, MI: Baker Book House, 1976.

Shea, Daniel B. *Spiritual Autobiography in Early America.* Princeton, NJ: Princeton University Press, 1968.

Trent, John. *Life Mapping.* Colorado Springs, CO: Focus on the Family Publishing, 1994.

Wakefield, Dan. *The Story of Your Life: Writing a Spiritual Autobiography.* Boston: Beacon Press, 1990.

Weibe, Katie Funk. *Good Times With Old Times: How to Write Your Memoirs.* Scottdale, PA: Herald Press, 1979.

Spiritual Autobiographies: A Sample

Buechner, Frederick. *Sacred Journey: A Memoir of Early Years.* San Francisco: HarperCollins, 1982.

Colson, Charles. *Born Again.* Old Tappan, NJ: Chosen Books/Fleming H. Revell, 1976.

Griffin, Emilie. *Turning: Reflections on the Experience of Conversion.* New York: Harper & Row, 1984.

Jones, E. Stanley. *A Song of Ascents.* Nashville, TN: Abingdon Press, 1972.

Lee, D. John, ed. *Storying Ourselves: A Narrative Perspective on Christians in Psychology.* Grand Rapids, MI: Baker Books, 1993.

Lewis, C. S. *Surprised by Joy: The Shape of My Early Life.* New York: Harcourt Brace Jovanovich, 1956.

Merton, Thomas. *Seven Storey Mountain.* New York: Harcourt Brace Jovanovich, 1948.

Wakefield, Dan. *Returning: A Spiritual Journey.* New York: Penguin Books, 1988.

Weibe, Katie Funk. *Border Crossing: A Spiritual Journey.* Scottdale, PA: Herald Press, 1995.

Books about the Discipline of Noticing

Bockmuehl, Klaus. *Listening to the God who Speaks: Reflections on God's Guidance from Scripture and the Lives of God's People.* Colorado Springs, CO: Helmers & Howard, Inc., 1990.

Edwards, Tilden. *Living in the Presence: Disciplines for the Spiritual Heart.* San Francisco: HarperSanFrancisco, 1987.

Huggett, Joyce. *Listening to God.* London: Hodder & Stoughton, 1986.

Payne, Leanne. *Listening Prayer: Learning to Hear God's Voice and Keep a Prayer Journal.* Grand Rapids, MI: Baker Books, 1994.

Pytches, David. *Does God Speak Today?* Minneapolis, MN: Bethany House Publishers, 1989.

Willard, Dallas. *In Search of Guidance: Developing a Conversational Relationship with God.* San Francisco: HarperSanFrancisco, 1993.